RAISING AN AUTISTIC GIRL: MODERN ASD STRATEGIES FOR SUCCESSFUL PARENTING

HELP YOUR CHILD SUCCEED IN A NEUROTYPICAL WORLD FOR A LIFE OF SUCCESS ON THE SPECTRUM (5–11-YEAR-OLDS)

TAYLOR EBERSTADT

CONTENTS

INTRODUCTION

On my thirtieth birthday, I decided to give myself one of the most meaningful gifts of my life: my diagnosis of Autism. The questions, evaluations, and observations of the mental health professional who assessed me led to a firm and clear diagnosis; one that I somehow always knew pertained to me. To this day, I wonder how receiving an earlier diagnosis could have changed my childhood and teen years.

Within the Autism community, there has always been a debate about how useful early diagnosis is. On the one hand, it is a huge relief to understand why you are different and why the things that seem so easy for others pose such an insurmountable obstacle for you. On the other hand, many parents justifiably fear that a diagnosis of Autism will lead their child to be stigmatized, judged, and isolated.

Receiving my diagnosis felt like breathing for the first time. I wept when I received my results because it was a confirmation that an idea I had always had in the back of my mind—that I was an awful person —was unfounded. There was a reason for all I had been through, and there was hope that my diagnosis could help me understand my place in the world a little better.

As I drove home from my doctor's office, a myriad of childhood memories flashed before my eyes. I journeyed through some of the most significant. My earliest memory of realizing I was a little different was when I struggled to make friends. I would watch other kids play and not know how to join or talk to them in a way that would make them want to keep playing with me. I learned how to mimic how they behaved, but only had one friend. Playing with more than one child at a time was very confusing; there was always just too much going on.

Having a diagnosis helped me understand why I felt so drained after interacting with other kids. Sensory overload was just one piece of the puzzle. A second obstacle was emotional regulation, which as a child was practically non-existent for me. I raged very, very quickly and because I wasn't allowed to self-soothe or have meltdowns, I learned different ways to regulate.

Competitive track running, mountain biking, boxing, lifting weights, and physically extreme sports like roller derby and Krav Maga were my lifesavers. These activities tired me out to such an extent that I had no energy left for outbursts. After hours of pushing myself to my limit, I would lie on my bed, my body exhausted but my mind racing —something that often happened when I felt overwhelmed. While these were all socially acceptable ways to self-regulate, they also became a means of self-harm. I wanted to feel something—anything— but constant "otherness."

My diagnosis explained all the many negative traits I had spent so long beating myself up about—my oversharing, not knowing how I felt, only wanting to talk about my interests, reaching my "people limit" very quickly, struggling to learn new things and understand explanations, raging when things didn't go the way I wanted. As it turns out, these behaviors all made up my version of Autism.

Today, I can't help but wonder how differently things would have gone if I had known I was Autistic. The constant sensation of being different from everyone else, my difficulties with figuring out social cues, the difficulties I had understanding what teachers were saying... all these differences eroded my self-esteem. Not being able to stim (calm myself) the way I needed to made it difficult for me to manage big emotions in a way that was healthy for me. In many ways, not having a diagnosis forced me to wear a mask for years when all I wanted was to be me.

Throughout my lifetime, I have worn various hats. I was a teacher for many years and also worked in the Army Reserves. Currently, I am a happily married, full-time mom of two daughters. Sometimes, when I watch my baby and toddler playing, my mind travels to the lives of other Autistic girls who may be struggling to find their place at school, with friends, and even within their own families. I can imagine that many are made to feel like they have to keep hiding their differences so that they can fit into a neurotypical world. My aim in this book is to share my insight and experiences with parents so that their child feels celebrated, acknowledged, and loved, just the way they are.

When I think of the many Autistic friends I have made along the way, I see that the one thing that all of those who are thriving have in common is self-acceptance. And that is why I created a signature framework for you, the reader of this book. It's called G.I.R.L.S. U.N.I.T.E.D. and it encapsulates everything I learned about Autism through my own experience and my extensive research. Each letter of this framework begins its own chapter and stands for one vital step in your journey as parents of an Autistic girl. Within these pages, you will find a blend of theoretical information and a vast array of exercises to put you in power of your parenting journey. I will start by sharing vital information on exactly what Autism is, highlighting common concurrent conditions and explaining the process of diagnosis.

Next, we will get straight to how to best support your daughter with daily, practical strategies. From sensory support right through help in academic pursuits and social interactions, the strategies and information you will find here are centered on ensuring your daughter builds the self-esteem she needs to see Autism as her unique power.

Some chapters will be devoted to helping you understand the many ways in which your child is trying to communicate with you. Others will center on why it is so important to foster your daughter's interests—they are a pillar of her self-esteem, and they may be one of the few ways in which she feels free to express herself, release pent-up energy, and connect with others who share her passions. We will also be delving into practical strategies, including tips for home design that can make life considerably smoother for your child and, indeed, your whole family. But I've saved the best for last! The last chapter may not be the only thing you need to be a confident parent to your Autistic girl, but for me, it is the very cornerstone of what I craved all my life: to be told that the very best thing I could be was myself. If everyone else is trying to get your daughter to do and say what they deem acceptable, then they've got it all wrong. No child should have to sacrifice her identity to be welcomed. If the world wants to change your child, make the universe change for her.

Ⓖ: GRASPING AUTISM

WHAT AUTISM IS AND WHAT IT ISN'T

> *"I am different, not less."*
>
> — DR. TEMPLE GRANDIN (ROSSON & WEEKS 2018)

For a parent—and a child—to be fully empowered, gaining as much knowledge as possible about Autism is vital. Doing so allows you to know what to expect and explains the thoughts, behaviors, and ways of seeing the world that can perplex your daughter and lead her to question her differences. It also gives you the courage to find ways—most importantly, *your* way—to discover more about yourself and the extent to which you are willing to raise your daughter in alignment with your values.

One story that I find particularly inspirational is that of Emily Grodin —a young Autistic woman who took twenty-five years to find her voice, and who hasn't stopped sharing her thoughts and emotions since. Emily had non-verbal Autism, which led her to miss out on many education and social opportunities and triggered numerous meltdowns. Her parents knew in their hearts that there was more to their daughter than was apparent on the surface. For instance, Emily would give them a gentle poke if they missed a word while reading her books, and at age five, she completed a 500-piece puzzle. Emily's mom, Valerie, fought tooth and nail to give her daughter the best education possible, to the point that she harnessed the knowledge she had gained from years working as an attorney to become a legal advocate for Autism (Miller 2021).

Eventually, the Grodin family found an approach that opened up a new world for Emily—Facilitated Communication (FC)—which involves a facilitator holding an Autistic person's hands, wrists, or arms, to help them spell messages on a keyboard or board with printed letters. FC, which was founded in Australia in the 1970s, postulates that Autism is mostly a movement disorder rather than one involving social and communication challenges. By offering physical assistance and emotional encouragement, a facilitator can help an Autistic person communicate. The American Psychological Association, the American Academy of Pediatrics, Speech Pathology Australia, and other organizations have recommended that FC not be used because they claim it can lead people with independent communication skills to become more passive communicators. They believe that the facilitator (not the Autistic person) writes the messages (often unconsciously), and postulate that children are better off receiving specialized schooling.

For Emily, however, FC made all the difference. From the outset, it was clear that she was doing her own writing, covering topics such as her medication and Jewish observances—subjects her facilitator knew nothing about. She wrote, "I have been buried under years of dust, and now I have so much to say," a statement which contradicts the view of Autistic people as literal thinkers. This sentence became the title of a memoir written by Emily and her mother.

Throughout your journey as a parent of a child with Autism, you will undoubtedly come across contrasting viewpoints concerning everything from chosen therapies to terminology. For instance, some people (including myself) choose to say "Autistic person" or "on the

Autism spectrum" instead of "person with Autism." I prefer the term Autistic, which is identity-first rather than person-first. Those of us who use this term feel that we do not need reminders that we are people, and we feel that Autism colors the entirety of our experience. Autism is not a source of shame or a second thought (Pittsburgh Center for Autistic Advocacy 2024). We capitalize the words Autistic and Autism in the same way that the Deaf community uses the big D to refer to culture. Capitalizing our A is a means of reflecting the unique culture shared by Autistic people involved in the Autistic Rights Movement.

Despite our different experiences, views, and preferences, one thing that Autistic people are lucky to share is information. We now know that masking who we are, stopping ourselves from self-soothing, and trying to conform to neurotypical expectations prevents us from being our biggest, boldest, happiest selves. Let's start, then, by looking at exactly what Autism is. Information is power and united, we can advocate for our freedom and individuality.

WHAT IS AUTISM?

Autism Spectrum Disorder (ASD) is a neurological and developmental disorder caused by differences in the brain. Autistic people often have difficulties in areas such as social communication and interaction, and they may have repetitive and/or restrictive behaviors and interests in specific topics or activities. From the medical and legal viewpoints, Autism is considered a disability. Those who meet specific criteria can qualify for government aid such as Supplemental Security Income (SSI).

ASD manifests itself in the following ways:

SOCIAL COMMUNICATION AND INTERACTION SKILLS

Autistic people may avoid maintaining eye contact, use fewer gestures (such as waving hello or goodbye) by the age of twelve months, and not point at things they are interested in by the age of eighteen months. By the time they are around two years old, they may not display typical reactions when someone is upset. It is vital to keep in mind that girls may be far more efficient at "masking." Therefore, they may study others and learn how to maintain eye contact even though it makes them uncomfortable. Sometimes, the amount of eye contact your daughter displays will depend on context.

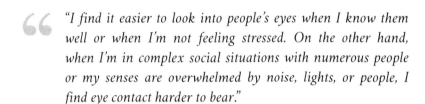

> *"I find it easier to look into people's eyes when I know them well or when I'm not feeling stressed. On the other hand, when I'm in complex social situations with numerous people or my senses are overwhelmed by noise, lights, or people, I find eye contact harder to bear."*

> — JANINA, 32

> *"I wish that more people knew that we find it tough to make out body language, including messages sent through the eyes. And coordinating two sources of sensory input can be a nightmare."*

> — SOFIA, 19

> *"I remember when I was at school, I used to walk up and down the classroom while my teacher was explaining something. She told my mom she was shocked that I was able to repeat everything she said.*

She assumed that I wasn't paying any attention to her at all because I wasn't looking at her."

— AUBREY, 29

UNIQUE INTERESTS AND REPETITIVE BEHAVIORS

As your daughter progresses from babyhood to toddlerhood and then childhood, you may notice that she displays specific behaviors. These can include:

- Focusing on specifics rather than the big picture.
- Being upset by small changes in their routine (sensory processing differences can make them hypersensitive or hyposensitive to sensory information). These sensitivities can cause them to feel overwhelmed in unfamiliar environments, resulting in anxiety and resistance to change (Hands Center for Autism 2024).
- Having a deep interest in parts of objects (some Autistic people enjoy taking things apart and putting them back together).
- Playing with toys the same way every time or preferring to partake in the same activity rather than try out new ones.
- Stimming (also called self-soothing, stimming can consist of hand flapping, rocking repeating words and phrases, spinning, and other behaviors).
- Echolalia (spontaneously repeating words or phrases or repeating phrases someone has said).
- Seemingly inattentive behavior (inattention in Autistic people often arises from sensory overload).
- Specific eating habits (Autistic kids often express a strong preference for foods that feel a certain way in their mouths. Some prefer soft, smooth foods like ice cream or soup, while others enjoy the stimulation of crunchy foods like carrots or chips).

- Specific sleeping habits (your child may have irregular sleeping and waking patterns, or they may sleep less than is expected for their age or remain awake for an hour or longer at nighttime).

"My daughter, Lara, would repeat sequences of numbers out loud during a conversation that had nothing to do with math, or take a phrase that someone had just used and repeat it many times over (echolalia)."

— DIEGO, 49

LANGUAGE SKILLS

Some children with ASD may not be able to communicate verbally, and some may have limited speaking skills. Others may have rich vocabularies and be able to discuss specific subjects in great detail. Many may find it hard to work out the meaning and rhythm of words and sentences and struggle to understand non-verbal language and vocal tone. They may show an uneven progression in language, developing a large vocabulary in one particular area of interest very quickly. Some kids have excellent memories, and others can read at a younger age than their peers. However, they may not be able to understand what these words mean.

"When I was at primary school, my teachers sometimes got angry at me for seeming inattentive or uninterested in what they were saying. I found eye contact challenging and because I didn't look at them when they were speaking, they thought I was being rude. When the tension would get too high, I would have a meltdown, and they complained many times to my parents about my emotional regulation issues."

— MICHELLE, 23

LEARNING SKILLS

Some ways in which Autism can affect learning include social skills impairment, difficulties with processing information and sensory input, communication challenges, and high anxiety levels. One issue that can impact learning is auditory processing disorder, which refers to brain-related difficulties with processing sounds in the brain.

To get an idea of what this feels like, imagine that you're chatting with a friend at a party. There is laughter, music, and other noises at different levels. As hard as you try to separate your friend's speech from all the other sounds, it is impossible. Now imagine you have to face this situation everywhere you go. Logically, the noisier your surroundings are, the harder it will be to process specific messages. Research shows that Autism and auditory processing disorders overlap, with parents' reports indicating that up to 80 percent of Autistic kids process sounds atypically (Schwartz n.d.).

MOVEMENT SKILLS

Research has consistently shown that Autistic kids have gross and fine motor delays and/or atypical motor patterns. They can have difficulties with posture, coordination, and motor planning. One study, for instance, has found that they obtain lower scores in praxis tests (which measure a person's ability to conceptualize, plan, and coordinate movements so they can carry out a motor task). There are various theories as to why motor difficulties are so prevalent among Autistic children. They include differences in brain wiring; joining hypermobility or low muscle tone; differences in body awareness, coordination, and praxis; and anxiety (which affects their willingness to take part in new or challenging tasks).

 "As a child, I had balance issues and had frequent falls and injuries as a result. My parents were relentless when it came to finding activities that would strengthen my gross motor

skills. They enrolled me in a few activities, including trampolining and swimming. At home, Dad would play lots of games with me, and I never knew they were targeted at improving my balance. My favorite game was pretending we were different kinds of animals and jumping, leaping, and standing on tip-toe, depending on the animal we were copying."

— ELIA, 54

SELF-ESTEEM ISSUES IN AUTISTIC GIRLS

Far more boys than girls receive an Autism diagnosis. Because Autism in girls may look different from how it manifests itself in boys, doctors may fail to diagnose it. Stereotypes abound about what Autism looks like, with many associating this disability with boys and trains. Yet girls may have a deep interest in a different subject (for instance, dogs, celebrities, or fantasy stories) and their behavior may be classified as typical and not meriting consideration for diagnosis. Add our ability to mask more efficiently into the equation, and it becomes easy to see why so many women like me are diagnosed when we are in our twenties, thirties, or later. As a result, many of us grow up thinking that there is something wrong with us and that we are hopeless or unlikeable. One negative interaction after another can quickly erode our self-esteem.

WHY MORE BOYS ARE DIAGNOSED THAN GIRLS

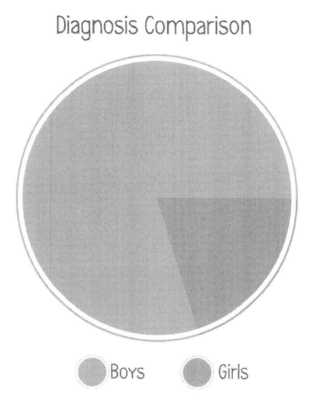

There are additional reasons other than our ability at masking that lead to lower rates of diagnosis in girls. Currently, boys are still diagnosed at a rate of 4:1 compared to girls, and it is mainly because the criteria for diagnosis are based on the typical presentation of this disorder in boys. For instance, girls tend to have a more advanced vocabulary than boys do. Meanwhile, boys tend to score lower on motor skills tests than girls. They tend to have less dexterity and balance than girls at a preschool age. However, girls may present motor skills issues later in life.

The Diagnostic and Statistical Manual of Mental Disorders, 5th edition, text revision (DSM-5-TR) does not differentiate between the symptoms of ASD in boys and girls. Their list of symptoms is as follows:

- persistent difficulties in social interactions
- trouble with social-emotional reciprocity
- deficits with non-verbal communication (including difficulties understanding non-verbal signals like facial expressions, tone of voice, and body language, and may find it hard to make eye contact)
- challenges in developing, maintaining, and understanding relationships
- repetitive interests and fixations
- difficulty dealing with unpredictability
- repetitive motor movements
- hyporeactivity or hyperreactivity to sensory input
- strict adherence to routines

It is worthwhile noting that not all Autistic people find it hard to make eye contact; in fact, some may be able to maintain eye contact or stare at the people they are interacting with. The difference between Autistic and neurotypical people lies in the understanding that looking into someone's eyes is a means of communicating. Autistic people may not see the usefulness of this means of communication. They may teach themselves to replicate this social norm without feeling it is particularly beneficial.

Also noteworthy is the fact that language, once a part of the diagnostic criteria for ASDs, has been dropped. This is because people with Autism vary greatly in their ability to speak and understand language. Author Sarah Hendrickx, for instance, had an IQ of 153 and spoke full sentences at the age of nine months. She was frequently labeled as "clever but lazy" at school (National Autistic Society 2019).

Some Autistic girls remain silent throughout their lives, while others are very chatty. Autistic kids can have a very wide vocabulary for their age and express themselves eloquently. Some may use complex vocabulary that neurotypical kids would not usually use.

The lower Autism diagnosis rate for girls suggests that amendment of the criteria may be warranted to take into account that girls may present differences in areas like social interaction. As mentioned, the tools used for diagnosis and screening are mainly based on data obtained from boys. They fail to account for the variations in Autism characteristics across the sexes.

One 2020 review indicates that two theories govern the reason behind lower diagnoses in females (Moore 2023). The first is the "female protective theory," which suggests that girls and women are biologically shielded from Autism. Some lab tests seem to support this theory. For instance, female mice with a deletion in the 16p11.2 chromosomal region, which is linked to ASD, do not have the learning problems shown by male mice with this deletion. They seem to compensate for the loss through a protein called ERK. Scientists have also observed that many sisters of boys with Autism don't develop Autism. Some researchers believe that there may be a factor in female development that helps them avoid the disorder (Williamson 2023). The second theory states that bias during diagnosis (looking out for typical male signs instead of accounting for differences between male and female behavior) is to blame.

GENDER DIFFERENCES

As a parent, it pays to be aware of traits that are more associated with female rather than male Autism. In the book *Unmasking Autism*, writer Devon Price (2022) divides the traits displayed by Autistic girls into four categories: emotional, psychological, behavioral, and social traits and behaviors. Boys may display some of these behaviors, too, including having difficulty identifying irony and sarcasm or understanding complex instructions. Like girls, boys can also be blunt and honest—a trait that can persist regardless of age.

Emotional:

- Girls may seem more immature than their neurotypical peers and may be perceived as highly sensitive
- They may cry or have meltdowns about seemingly unimportant matters
- They find it hard to recognize or identify their emotions
- They may feel overwhelmed when somebody else is upset, but not be sure how to support them
- They may seem to lack energy after socializing with others or being in stimulating environments

Psychological:

- They can experience anxiety and social anxiety
- They can seem moody or depressed to others
- They may have been diagnosed with mood disorders (including BPD or narcissistic personality disorder) before receiving an Autism diagnosis
- They may seem very insecure and eager to be accepted by others
- They may feel very hurt if they think others have a low opinion of them

Behavioral:

- They may impose very strict rules on themselves/aim to control themselves and their environment to deal with stress
- They are usually most comfortable at home or in familiar environments
- They may seem young for their age owing to their fashion sense, interests, or behaviors

- They may exercise excessively and/or count calories or restrict their diet as a means to deal with stress and have a body type that conforms to standard expectations
- They may attempt to self-soothe by listening to the same music over and over, twirling their hair, picking at skin, fidgeting, and similar
- They may not enjoy playing with typical "girls' toys"
- They may seem more logical and pragmatic (and less socially intuitive) than neurotypical girls, even though some may enjoy playing with dolls and wearing pink
- They may display what others see as "boyish" behavior
- They may not identify with behaviors typically displayed by girls, even at a very young age
- They may not enjoy being hugged
- They may have aversions to some textures and fabrics
- They may intensely dislike specific foods and have very defined preferences
- They may be intolerant of or allergic to one or more foods
- They can be perfectionists
- They can be hesitant to ask for help

Social:

- They may be very adept at changing to fit in with the group they are in
- They may have just one close friend or an imaginary friend
- They may prefer friendship with one or more boys because they find male friendship dynamics easier to understand
- They may struggle with the social side of school, college, or work
- They may be quiet or shy but become loquacious when discussing a subject that interests them
- They may not start conversations but appear extroverted when approached

- They may find it easier to talk about shallow topics than connect with someone on a deeper level
- They may fear disappointing someone or disagreeing with them while having a conversation
- They may not tolerate sharing during play and may become angry with those who try to take their toys or possessions
- When playing with others, they may either insist that all games be played on their terms or play a more passive role, letting more socially adept girls take the lead

Research by Attwood indicates that during the elementary school years, Autistic boys tend to prefer playing alone, at some distance from their classmates. Girls, meanwhile, tend to stick close to their peers, weaving in and out of activities. This may camouflage their social difficulty and make them harder for parents and teachers to spot.

 "When I turned 13, I became obsessed with counting calories. I found it hard to make friends and thought that if at least I could look slim, then I wouldn't call attention to myself and others wouldn't tease me for being different."

— SANDRA, 42

 "I had just one good friend in high school, but have many friends online from the gaming community. I find that gaming is my biggest source of stress-relief, and it is relieving to find other people who could talk for hours about my favorite games."

— SAVANNAH, 28

PREFERRED ACTIVITIES AND SPECIAL INTERESTS

One 2009 study tested 157 boys and forty-two girls with ASD (aged 1.5 to 3.9 years of age), and found that girls had greater difficulties in the communication domain, while boys had more restricted/repetitive/stereotyped interests and behaviors (Hartley and Sikora 2009). Hendrickx (2015), on the other hand, has found that while girls' behavior can be restrictive and repetitive, the type of activity varies. For instance, they tend to favor activities such as watching visual content repeatedly, reading the same book, and learning scripts and lyrics by heart. They also enjoy collecting and sorting items (including Lego), and their interests tend to be people- rather than object-based and/or involve some type of language or communication.

Research by Attwood (2007), meanwhile, has revealed that Autistic girls may have special interests that are considered typical for girls their age. These include TV shows or social media channels, collecting dolls, riding horses, or following celebrities or influencers. Their choices appear to be linked to camouflage and imitating behavior, making it harder to identify "special interests," as required by the DSM-5. Their interests may also center around animals, nature, stuffed toys, historical characters, and collecting items. Research by Knickmeyer et al. (2008) showed that Autistic girls and boys prefer games that do not require pretense or imagination.

When playing games that do not involve pretense, they prefer games that are not typically "female." These include transport and construction games such as Lego, playing with robots, and similar. Even when they play with soft toys, their activities tend to involve collecting and organizing instead of imagination (Hendrickx, 2015). However, when playing "pretend" games, they do show a preference for typically female toys and games. Researchers hypothesize that this could be because they learn to play this type of game from their parents. What's more, girls may take part in this type of play to fit in.

Autistic girls may have a deep interest in fantasy and/or have an imaginary friend. In one recent study (Davis et al. 2023), 50 percent of kids taking part had an imaginary friend. These children displayed better social skills, displaying an enhanced understanding of the mental and emotional states of others.

GENDER TYPICALITY

Research indicates that females with Autism have a more masculinized or androgynous neurological profile than neurotypical females (Hendrickx, 2015). Moreover, studies reveal that Autistic natal females (those born as biological females) are prone to lower affiliation to a gender group and greater variance in their gender expression. There are two possible explanations for this finding. The first is that because there is greater gender diversity among Autistic natal females, it can be harder to choose one group to identify with. The second is that they may have selected a gender group to identify with but found it had to interact with the members of this group. Research also shows that Autistic natal females report lower femininity and higher masculinity than Autistic males. Studies have also shown that Autistic females may have a preference for socializing with men.

In general, Autism is a condition with high levels of gender variance, both in males and females. People with Autism are less likely to identify with a specific gender group than allistics, and they tend to view their gender groups more negatively. This finding is important because gender identification and self-esteem are linked to psychological well-being in neurotypical females and males.

When discussing gender, it is vital to be aware of the fact that the label "female Autism" fails to take into account that a high percentage of Autistic people are transgender and non-conforming. Moreover, as observed by Price (2022), there may be high percentages of Autistic transgender youth because Autistic people are less likely to succumb to the social pressures that stop neurotypical transgender people from coming out.

THE DANGER OF STEREOTYPING

Stereotyping Autism (for instance, assuming that all Autistic people like math or trains and are unable to make friends) can be harmful to girls and can result in a later diagnosis, as found in a study by Bargiela et al. (2016). The latter found that the Autistic difficulties of girls are often ignored or misunderstood. As a result, many women report having experienced anxiety, depression, and eating disorders. Many are treated for this condition for years without the subject of Autism being brought up. What's more, even when Autistic women have approached health professionals with suspicions that they might have ASD, their concerns were often dismissed. Many have been misdiagnosed with everything from BPD to multiple personality disorder.

"I tried so hard to fit in that nobody realized anything was wrong. Sometimes I wish that I had 'misbehaved' so that at least someone would realize how difficult school and getting on with others was."

— MARGIE, 18

"I was bullied by a group of girls and when I told my teacher, she told me I should behave more normally."

— SASHA, 34

"I avoided disagreeing with others at all costs because I didn't want to be seen as different or difficult. I had one friend at school and sometimes, I couldn't hold it in, and I would just be my blunt self with her, and she would tell me I was hurtful."

— LISA, 27

AUTISM AND SEXUAL ASSAULT

Autistic girls have a dramatically higher risk of being sexually assaulted. One survey (Cazalis et al. 2022) found that nine Autistic women out of ten have been victims of sexual violence. Specifically, being Autistic means having a 10–16 percent risk of enduring sexual molestation as a child and a 62 percent risk of being sexually victimized in adulthood. Most victims are girls and women. Autistic females have a risk of being sexually assaulted that is two to three times higher than females who are not on the spectrum. Some 77 percent of participants had only experienced heterosexual sex over their lifetime, despite the high percentage of declared queer orientations (71.6 percent). The authors stated that this gap could be explained by factors such as cultural stereotypes, a lower proportion of potential partners, and Autistic characteristics such as masking and social imitation strategies. The researchers concluded that since 60.1 percent of participants were bisexual, they may have simply settled for the most available type of relationship.

The survey found that both sexual victimization and revictimization were very high. For some participants, victimization occurred as a child, teen, and adult. Being young made things worse, as it was a significant factor in later-life revictimization. Researchers have also found that Autistic girls enter puberty significantly earlier than non-Autistic girls, putting them at an even greater risk. As found in a study by Skoog and Özdemir (2015), "early maturing girls are sexually harassed as a result of natural and normative sexual development, which happens earlier than for most of their peers."

The researchers concluded that it is not Autism itself or social communication challenges that increase Autistic girls' and women's vulnerability to sexual violence. Instead, it is the fact that they are perceived as different. This reflects research showing that women with Attention Deficit Hyperactivity Disorder (ADHD) also have a high risk of being victimized. Perpetrators of sexual violence either manipulate or harass their victims or take them by surprise. As written by Roberts et al. (2015), Autistic victims of sexual assault have deficits in emotional and social cognition that make them unable to identify sexually inappropriate behavior or to identify their discomfort. Four out of ten victims felt that being aware of risks and utilizing self-affirmation strategies could have prevented the assault. However, because assault can take place in a girl's childhood, it is equally vital to prevent them from being in situations in which they can be taken advantage of—and this is a priority not only for families but also for schools and governments. Sexual violence takes a huge toll on Autistic females' mental and physical health. For one out of five women surveyed, the most efficient protection is the presence of a vigilant caregiver. Families can benefit greatly from education about the risk of sexual assault of Autistic girls.

THE HARMS OF MASKING

When Autistic girls are encouraged to mask their behaviors so that others don't take notice of their disability, the ensuing harm is significant. Masking can lead them to be repeatedly misdiagnosed, it can erode their sense of identity, and it can push them into burnout and unhealthy behaviors. Autistic girls may spend an entire day masking at school, only to come home and have a massive meltdown owing to the effort of behaving as others expect all day. Many Autistic women do not feel that they can be themselves until significantly later in life (when they are in their thirties or even their forties). The role of families in making their children feel accepted and celebrated just as they are cannot be overstated. The Autism community would also benefit greatly from better representation in media, education the arts, research, and more avenues (McAllister 2020).

JOURNALING EXERCISE

Before moving on to Chapter Two, take your journal and write down your answers to the following questions. They are based on Tony

Attwood's screening test for Autistic girls and his advice on how to recognize the signs of Autism in females (Garnett and Attwood, n.d.).

1. Does your daughter choose single close friendships instead of being part of a group?
2. Do they prefer to have male friends?
3. Do they have special interests in celebrities, animals, literature, fantasy, or friendships?
4. Do they focus intensely on the interests in 3?
5. Do they use imaginative play to reenact real events?
6. Do they tend to follow scripts and rules and prefer to stick to routines?
7. Do they have difficulties recognizing and managing conflict, or find it hard to repair friendships after an argument?
8. Do they easily become overwhelmed in social situations?
9. Are they reluctant to take part in class activities?
10. Do you notice that they withdraw from social interactions?

In this chapter, we have seen that girls are often misdiagnosed or diagnosed later in life for Autism. While a diagnosis can have its pros and cons, it can undoubtedly help parents find vital help for their kids, setting them on a track to greater self-acceptance. Autistic girls have a higher risk of low self-esteem and sexual violence. Information is power when it comes to parenting. The earlier parents identify their daughter's struggles and needs, the sooner they can understand their child and refrain from encouraging masking behaviors that only harm their child and deprive them of their identity. In Chapter Two, we will move on to a topic that is closely related to diagnosis: concurrent conditions. For many Autistic girls, the road to a correct diagnosis may involve being diagnosed with one or more of the conditions covered in Chapter Two.

IDENTIFYING CO-EXISTING CONDITIONS

> *"I'm not broken. I'm different and that's okay."*
>
> — ELLEN HEDGER (MONGINA 2024)

Several medical or psychiatric conditions can exist alongside Autism; close to 76 percent of kids with Autism are diagnosed with a concurrent condition. Sometimes, these diagnoses are steps on the journey to receiving an Autism diagnosis. Concurrent conditions may appear during childhood, the teen years, or adulthood. It is vital to receive a separate diagnosis for them if they are present, so your child can receive the appropriate treatment. Below are a few conditions that can coexist with Autism (Raising Children n.d.).

ANXIETY

Between 40 and 60 percent of children with Autism also have anxiety, a disorder that causes symptoms such as worry, panic, hyperactivity, and restlessness. Autistic kids may also have social anxiety, which is an intense, persistent fear of being watched and judged by others.

The symptoms of anxiety in Autistic children include having emotional outbursts, sleep issues, the avoidance of social situations, and self-harming actions like biting or scratching oneself, or head-banging. When children are having a panic attack, they may feel faint, their hearts may start to race, and they may experience hyperventilation. If so, breathing into a paper bag can help restore the CO_2 that is lost when human beings take in too many short breaths (which can occur when they are anxious).

For kids with Autism, triggers for anxiety attacks include changes in their routine or environment, overwhelming or new social situations, having a fear of a particular situation or thing (for instance, balloons or sleeping alone), and key transitions in life (including the transition from grade school to middle school, or the onset of puberty).

Although boys are significantly more likely to be diagnosed with Autism, girls are more likely to experience anxiety with their disorder. In one 2023 study, 112 kids with Autism (eighty-nine boys and twenty-three girls) had brain scans when they were toddlers and at three other points in their lives (Aherne 2023). Their parents were interviewed about anxiety when their kids were aged nine to eleven. The results showed that girls had higher anxiety rates than boys, particularly in presentations of this disorder that are closely related to Autism (including the fear of change). They also had higher rates of traditional anxieties, including generalized anxiety, social anxiety, and separation anxiety than boys. Those with Autism-related anxiety had slower growth in the brain's fear center (the amygdala) while those with traditional anxieties had a larger right amygdala than kids without anxiety.

Because kids with Autism can, as a whole, be resistant to changes in their routine, anxiety can sometimes be hard to spot. The researchers noted that the difference may lie in when anxiety manifests itself. For instance, kids with Autism are usually afraid of change and can react when they are subjected to unexpected circumstances. Those with anxiety, on the other hand, have anticipatory worry—meaning they worry even before they are subjected to change (Mann 2023).

To deal with your Autistic daughter's anxiety, try natural calming methods such as breathwork, exercises, time spent in the Great Outdoors, going to a quiet part of your home, and taking part in activities they enjoy. If your child is struggling with anxiety, a professional therapist can help them quell their symptoms through approaches such as cognitive behavioral therapy, social stories (stories that prepare your child for stressful or new situations), exposure therapy, relaxation techniques, and more.

ATTENTION DEFICIT HYPERACTIVITY DISORDER (ADHD)

There is a strong link between ADHD and Autism, with statistics showing that around 40 percent of Autistic people have ADHD (some studies suggest that this figure could be as high as 70 percent). Moreover, between 20 percent and 50 percent of people with ADHD are Autistic. Both ASD and ADHD are classified as neurodevelopmental disorders in the DSM-5, and they share many common traits. These include atypical movement (such as stimming), inattentiveness, social difficulties, and learning style differences. People with either or both of these disorders can also display sensory sensitivities (Marschall 2024). Because traits can be similar, it is more difficult for people with ADHD to obtain a diagnosis of Autism.

Typically, assessments are only made for one of these two diagnoses simultaneously, so obtaining separate diagnoses for both may be useful. In the next chapter, we will discuss the process of diagnosing Autism. For now, it pays to know that professionals use different tools to diagnose ADHD and Autism. For ADHD, professionals often use rating scales such as the Conners Rating Scale, as well as attention tests and the Behavior Rating Inventory of Executive Functioning. The latter seeks to provide data on the extent to which executive dysfunction (an inability to manage one's thoughts, emotions, and actions) impacts a child in their day-to-day life.

Treatment for ADHD usually involves medication, while children with ASD may respond better to behavior therapy, which focuses on teaching them the skills they need to cope with daily life and manage issues such as sensory overload. Medication for ADHD can lead to lesser appetite. Kids with ASD can have nutritional gaps owing to sensory issues, which is why paying attention to diet in the case of both disorders is key (CHADD, n.d.).

BIPOLAR DISORDER (BPD)

Studies indicate that bipolar disorder (BPD) may be quite common among kids and adults with Autism, with as many as 27 percent of Autistic kids also having BPD symptoms (Hellings and Witwer, n.d.) and around 40 percent of people with BPD also exhibiting Autistic traits. Recent studies have also found a link between Autism and several mental illnesses, including schizophrenia. Interestingly, many neurodiversity specialists believe that conditions such as schizophrenia, BPD, OCD, and PTSD could all be different types of neurodivergence. Some Autistic people have symptoms of bipolar, including problems with sleep, agitation, impulsivity, and hyperactivity. When Autistic people are non-verbal, it can be difficult to distinguish their Autism from bipolar traits.

There are differences that specialists use to distinguish between the two disorders during a diagnosis. For instance, BPD tends to manifest itself in mood cycles between mania and depression and may not result in communication-related Autistic traits. ASD, on the other hand, often occurs alongside depression. Diagnosticians typically look for specific behavioral differences when checking for Autism. These include speech delays and/or echolalia, stimming, lack of eye contact, sensory dysfunction, and communication support needs (Rudy 2023). As mentioned, however, in girls, these traits may be harder to pinpoint, even for seasoned professionals.

DEPRESSION

Autistic people are four times more likely to develop depression than neurotypical people. Indeed, depression is considered the most common mental health condition among those on the Autism spectrum (Ruggieri 2020). However, it can be challenging to obtain a diagnosis for depression, because this condition can manifest itself differently in Autistic people. For instance, a person on the spectrum may not show symptoms like sadness, but rather, be restless or have insomnia. Parents and health professionals need to be attentive to these symptoms rather than attributing all behavioral issues to Autism.

A recent study published in the journal, *Research in Autism Spectrum Disorders* revealed that there are specific risk factors involving thinking of suicide and suicide attempts in Autistic kids. In the study, the percentage of kids rated by their parents as thinking about (or attempting) suicide from "sometimes" to "very often" was twenty-eight times greater in Autistic than in neurotypical children. However, it was three times less in Autistic kids than in non-Autistic kids with depression (McDougle, n.d.).

Suicidal ideation is uncommon in kids aged under ten. However, these statistics indicate the importance of clinicians assessing their patients when evaluating them for ASD. It is important for them to speak to parents, educators, and other adults who spend time with their patients.

SIGNS INDICATING THAT AN AUTISTIC CHILD MAY HAVE DEPRESSION

The causes of depression vary from experiencing traumatic events to lacking support or even having alexithymia (difficulties with identifying, understanding, and managing emotions). As mentioned above, signs of depression may be different in Autistic girls and boys. In addition to insomnia and restlessness, however, it also pays to watch out for:

- Persistent sadness or hopelessness
- Sleeping too much or too little
- A loss of interest in things they used to enjoy
- Eating much more or less than usual
- Frequently complaining of headaches, tummy aches, and discomfort
- A feeling of worthlessness
- Thoughts of self-harm or suicide
- Changes in appetite or weight
- Changes in energy levels
- Avoiding contact with others
- Social withdrawal
- An increase in repetitive behaviors
- More frequent or intense meltdowns

THE PAIN OF FEELING DIFFERENT FROM OTHERS

Many adults with Autism recall their childhood with sadness, since they may never have felt that they belonged, no matter how hard they tried. This sense of sticking out and feeling lonely can become stronger in middle school, when the teen identity begins to form and kids want more than anything else to be accepted by others. Moreover, Autistic children are more likely to be bullied than allistic kids, which can trigger sadness and depression.

As mentioned earlier, Autistic girls can be highly skilled at masking. Other people may not notice how hard they are trying to maintain eye contact, say "the right things" or simply avoid being identified as different, yet masking for hours on end can wear them out. As a result, they may have significant meltdowns, which can make them feel embarrassed, ashamed, and isolated. Others' judgment and bullying can make a child feel like their life is out of their control, and they may feel like things will never get better.

STRATEGIES FOR COPING WITH DEPRESSION

It is vital that Autistic girls with depression receive the help they need from trained professionals. Your child's doctor may recommend a therapist specializing in cognitive behavioral therapy (which helps kids reframe negative thoughts and beliefs by inviting them to let go of biases and look at available evidence). Therapists may also suggest approaches such as mindfulness training, emotional awareness training, and psychodynamic therapy (a type of talk therapy centered on learning how someone's subconscious thoughts, feelings, and memories affect their behavior).

In addition to seeking professional help, you can also embrace strategies such as (Bernard 2013):

- Listening keenly for any signs that your child may be having suicidal thoughts.
- Taking necessary steps to eliminate any bullying behavior your child may be facing at school.
- Giving your child opportunities to interact with other children.
- Watching out for any potential side effects of the medication she is taking.
- Ensuring she leads a healthy lifestyle comprising nutritious, whole foods, daily exercise, regular sleep, and mindful practices such as meditation, breathing, and spending time in nature.

EATING DISORDERS

There is also a notable link between Autism and eating disorders. One study (Parsons 2023) found, for instance, that some 27.5 percent of young women seeking treatment for an eating disorder had a high percentage of Autistic traits. Another study found a 23.3 percent Autism rate among young women seeking treatment for anorexia (Westwood, Mandy, and Tchanturia 2017).

The list of eating disorders that can be prevalent among Autistic people includes anorexia nervosa, binge-eating disorder, bulimia nervosa, and avoidant or restrictive food intake. You may find that your Autistic daughter refuses to eat specific foods. I, for instance, have a big aversion to fruit, one that began in my early childhood.

Some scientists believe that the relationship between Autistic traits and eating disorders can be partially attributed to alexithymia—an impaired ability to be aware of, explicitly identify, and describe one's feelings. Across the spectrum of eating disorders, people report having difficulties recognizing or describing their emotions. Alexithymia is more prevalent among females than males, and it can be present not only among Autistic people and neurotypical people with eating disorders, but also among those with OCD, PTSD, and schizophrenia (Westwood et al. 2017).

"I was always very particular about the foods I'd eat. I used to always have the same breakfasts in the summer (fruit smoothies) and in the colder months (oatmeal and fruit). Whenever I ate something different, I had GERD (gastrointestinal reflux) and felt like I was throwing up. I got used to throwing up after eating things that made me feel sick and when I was twelve, I began bingeing and purging. My parents found me a therapist and I learned that when we overeat, dopamine rewards us by releasing happy sensations. This can also happen when we restrict our diet or fast, which is why people with anorexia can feel good when they deprive themselves of food. I was also scared when I discovered that eating disorders can change your brain and affect your heart. I have a healthier relationship with food these days, but I do try to ensure that I stick to the foods that make me feel good."

— KATIE, 36

FOOD ALLERGIES AND INTOLERANCES

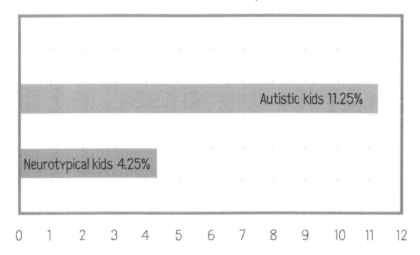

Prevalence of Food Allergies in
Autistic and Neurotypical Kids

Autistic kids 11.25%

Neurotypical kids 4.25%

0   1   2   3   4   5   6   7   8   9   10   11   12

Autistic kids may be more vulnerable to food intolerances and allergies because of digestive and immune system issues. Studies have shown that around 11.25 percent of Autistic kids have food allergies, compared to 4.25 percent of neurotypical kids. What's more, around 18.7 percent of Autistic children have respiratory allergies, compared to 12 percent of non-Autistic kids (Furfaro 2018).

Some doctors postulate that children with Autism may have "leaky gut syndrome," a condition that is thought to occur when large, intact protein molecules pass through the intestinal lining into the gut stream. Those who back this theory explain that when the digestive system functions optimally, the junctions between cells in the gastrointestinal wall are tight. They act as a barrier so that only small, single molecules like vitamins, minerals, and amino acids can make their way into the bloodstream. When leaky gut syndrome is present, the larger molecules in the bloodstream can cause the immune system to go haywire, because it identifies these molecules as foreign particles requiring an attack. As these proteins travel through the body, cells release an array of chemicals (including cytokines, interleukin, and histamine), which set off inflammation and a host of allergy symptoms.

In recent years, much research has been conducted into gut bacteria and Autism. Although research is still in its early stages, researchers have found differences in the gut microbiome (the ecosystem of microbes that live in the intestines) among Autistic children. Research is currently centered on discovering whether dietary changes could lead to changes in the gut microbiome that would benefit Autistic kids.

Currently, some parents are feeding gluten- and casein-free diets to their children. However, there does not seem to be evidence to support this dietary plan. What's more, avoiding nutritionally important foods may be detrimental to a child's health, which is why consulting with their doctor is always a good idea when it comes to their nutritional intake.

If your child has a food allergy, then they may have:

- Ear infections
- Nasal congestion, a runny nose, and/or sneezing
- Eyes issues such as teary or itchy eyes
- Swelling in the mouth, tongue, and throat
- Skin issues such as eczema and hives
- Respiratory issues like asthma and coughing
- Neurological issues like headaches and migraines
- Irritability, meltdowns, and hyperactivity

If you suspect your daughter has a food allergy, consider asking your healthcare provider for testing. They may recommend one of several tests to diagnose food allergies, including a skin prick test, blood test, elimination diet, and/or an oral food challenge.

SLEEP ISSUES

Over half of all children and adults with ASD have difficulties falling and/or staying asleep, with some studies indicating that the figure may exceed 80 percent. What's more, when Autistic kids fail to get good quality sleep, they have significantly more behavioral and learning issues. It has been found, for instance, that children who don't sleep for the required number of hours have more serious social issues, including interaction with peers. They can also have more compulsive reactions and/or have behaviors related to ADHD, depression, or OCD. There is also evidence that frequent night wakings can lead to behavioral dysregulation (Rudy 2023).

WHAT IS GOOD QUALITY SLEEP?

Healthy sleep involves both sleep quantity and sleep quality. Children need to sleep a certain number of hours depending on their age. For instance, toddlers need to sleep eleven to fourteen hours, while those aged six to twelve need just nine to twelve hours. Good sleep quality, meanwhile, involves falling asleep relatively quickly (within around half an hour of getting into bed), waking up no more than once during the night, and being awake for no longer than twenty minutes if one has woken up. When kids get good sleep quality, they feel refreshed when they wake up in the morning. When they don't, they can feel tired, sluggish, and find it hard to get out of bed.

WHY DO KIDS WITH AUTISM HAVE A HIGHER CHANCE OF HAVING SLEEP ISSUES?

The exact reason why children with Autism can struggle with sleep is as yet unknown, but one reason postulated for this issue is their sensory issues. Because they are highly sensitive to sounds and sensations, they may find it hard to filter these out during bedtime. Some studies indicate that Autistic people produce less melatonin at night than neurotypical people. Studies also suggest that treatment with melatonin seems to improve sleep disturbances in the majority of Autistic adults and kids (Carmassi et al. 2019). Some experts think that sleep issues in Autistic kids have genetic underpinnings. Others believe that physical and mental illnesses and conditions (including sleep apnea, OCD, anxiety, ADHD, and other issues) can all do their share to make sleep harder to come by.

STRATEGIES FOR BETTER SLEEP

To help your daughter sleep better at night, encourage her to embrace specific habits in the daytime, including exercising daily, avoiding excitement after around 3 p.m., and avoiding daytime naps once they are around five years of age. In the evening, ensure they stop using screens a few hours before bedtime, since screens can make them more alert and prevent them from feeling sleepy. Establish a nightly routine, which can include a bath, massage, bedtime story, and/or a meditation session. In Chapter Nine, you will find tips for bedroom design that can help your child enjoy quality sleep (Raising Children n.d.).

MINDFULNESS IS A POWERFUL TOOL

Mindfulness, a mental practice that involves being fully present "in the here and now," can help kids get better sleep, improve their social and emotional regulation skills, and boost their overall well-being. People who spend too much time ruminating over past events or worrying about the future can feel more stressed, anxious, and depressed. Mindfulness also involves accepting one's thoughts and emotions—even when they are tough or challenging. Because it fosters self-awareness, it can help Autistic girls with emotional regulation and communication so they can recognize what they are feeling and respond healthily.

Mindfulness isn't just for your child, though. Research has shown that parental mindfulness can boost the parent-child relationship. Studies on stress in mothers of Autistic children have found that mindfulness can act as a protective factor. If you find that you frequently feel stressed or overburdened, consider taking up mindful pursuits such as yoga, meditation, Tai Chi, and any exercise that captivates you. Some parents find attending skills-based parental training programs useful. These programs help parents alleviate their stress and enhance positive interactions with their children. Just a few resources that can point you in the right direction in terms of positive parenting and family-centered programs include Nationwide Children's (www.nationwidechildrens.org), Autism Speaks (www.Autismspeaks.org), and Stanford Medicine (www.med.stanford.edu/Autismcenter/EducationandTraining). Many offer online programs, so distance doesn't need to be an obstacle if you're interested in learning or updating your mindfulness and positive parenting strategies.

MINDFULNESS EXERCISES

Try these exercises with your daughter. They can come in handy when she is feeling stressed or anxious, or when she wishes to focus on her schoolwork.

Deep Breathing

Breathing is one of the most effective tools there is for nipping stress and anxiety in the bud. It helps to slow down the heart rate and induce a state of relaxation. There are many deep breathing exercises to choose from, and we have included a few of the most child-friendly techniques below. Try to have fun with it and use it as an opportunity to bond!

- **Blowing Bubbles**

A great way for girls to tap into the power of breathing is simply to learn how to exhale for a longer-than-usual period of time... and one very natural way of doing so is by blowing bubbles! Kids have to blow carefully and slowly, so you can start by inviting them to blow the biggest bubble they can.

- **Belly Breathing With a Favorite Toy**

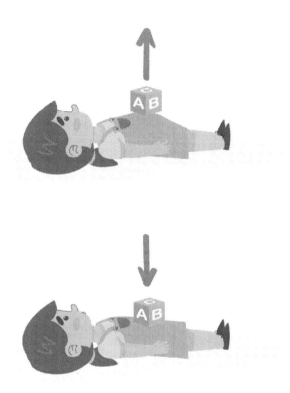

If your daughter has a toy she doesn't like separating herself from, then it will make the perfect prop to help her understand how belly breathing works. Ask her to lie on her back and place her toy over her belly button. Encourage her to breathe in and watch the toy rise upward, then breathe out and watch the toy drop. You can also introduce toys like Hoberman spheres into the equation. As she breathes in and her belly rises, pull the Hoberman sphere to the side so it becomes bigger. As she exhales, push the sphere inward so it becomes smaller.

- **Square Breathing**

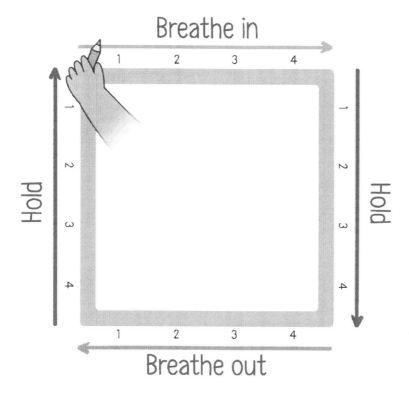

Adults call this "box breathing" and it involves counting to four while you go through your breathing exercises. In this case, your daughter can use drawing to hone this technique. Start with a simple drawing of a large square and place a piece of tracing paper above it. Ask your child to start at one point of the square. Ask her to breathe in for four counts as she draws the first side of the square, then hold her breath for four counts as she draws the second side. Next, ask her to exhale for four counts as she draws the third side of the square, and finally, to hold her breath for four counts as she draws the final side of the square.

- **Star Breathing**

This is another drawing exercise, though kids can also simply trace their fingers over the lines as they breathe. Start with a big A4 drawing of a five-pointed star. There are many free drawings of the breathing star online, so simply print one for greater ease and laminate it so it stands the test of time. As your child moves their finger up one side of the star, they breathe in for a count of three. When they come to a point, they hold their breath for a count of three. They then move down the second line and breathe out for a count of three, then hold for a count of three, and so on. They can make their way through the star various times if they wish.

Visualization

This technique involves helping a child focus on beautiful, calming images when they feel stressed or anxious. There are numerous visualization tools online for kids on sites like YouTube, but you can also make up your own visualization exercises, focusing on the things your child loves the most. For instance, if your daughter loves nature, then you might invite her to close her eyes and see the most beautiful flower in the world in her mind's eye. Ask her to focus on how large the flower is, how it connects to its stem, and what it feels like. Are there many petals or just a few? Invite them to put their imaginary flower to their nose. What does it smell like? As a follow-up activity, your child can draw their imaginary flower.

Another activity that can help kids who feel stressed or anxious is a popular exercise called **The Worry Tree**. For the visualization exercise, ask your daughter to close her eyes and imagine she is in a beautiful forest. There is a large, old tree there with many branches. Ask her to think of her worries and to pin each of her worries on one of the tree's branches. Then, ask her to sit in this beautiful forest and enjoy the silence and sense of peace. Tell her to imagine that a beautiful, friendly animal comes up to her. She caresses the animal, and they move to a beautiful sunny spot. They can return to the Worry Tree any time they want to, but they can simply enjoy the sun and explore other parts of the forest.

Yoga Sensory Activities

Many Autistic children have difficulty with sensory integration: spatial awareness, body awareness, and motor control. The practice of yoga can help them enhance their awareness of their bodies and hone their fine and gross motor skills. Yoga can also help kids enhance their motor planning—a skill that allows them to remember and carry out all the skills involved with a specific task. For example, when your daughter has a bath, she has to remember to open the bathroom cabinet to get her body gel, then apply a small amount on her bath sponge so that the bottle's entire contents don't flow out. Next, she has to squeeze the sponge so it absorbs the gel, then perform circles with the sponge on different parts of her body. She then has to rinse her body and the sponge and put everything back where it was. Phew! Those are many steps... and without motor planning, the task can seem insurmountable (Costello 2019). Just a few yoga poses that can enhance sensory integration include:

- **The Baby Cobra Pose**

This pose is easy and fun, and it can help ground and calm your child. Ask her to lie on her belly with her elbows bent and to place her hands under her shoulders. Next, encourage her to inhale air as she lifts her head, shoulders, and chest away from the floor, using her back muscles to lift her. Ask her to exhale with a "Hissss" and lower her back down to the floor. Ask her to repeat the exercise various times, inviting her to slowly extend the amount of time she inhales and exhales.

- **The Tree Pose**

This pose can help your child hone her balance and concentration, which can be difficult for those who have sensory processing issues. Ask her to stand with her feet hip-width apart, and to stretch her arms out to either side of her body, as though she were a tree. Next, ask her to gently raise her hands slightly higher and lift one foot off the ground, laying it flat against her other leg (beneath the knee). Ask her to freeze for three seconds and then congratulate her.

- **The Bridge Pose**

This pose can help your child hone the awareness of their body in space (proprioception). This ability allows you to do things like close your eyes and touch your nose with your index finger, or know if your feet are standing on hard cement or a soft surface without looking. It also allows you to do things like balance on one leg or throw a ball without looking at the arm that's throwing it.

In Autistic people, proprioceptive difficulties may contribute to decreased motor planning and postural control. The Bridge can help hone this awareness because it involves squeezing the major core muscles and placing pressure on the shoulders, head, and feet on the ground. To help your daughter perform this pose, ask her to lie flat on her back with her knees bent and her heels under her knees. Next, ask her to lift her butt off the ground and tilt her torso until the weight falls to her shoulders. Her arms should be flat and slightly under her back and her hands, facing palms-down. Ask her to take a few deep breaths then lower her body to the ground (Grogan 2023).

Many more yoga activities can hone proprioception and other sensory capacities so if your daughter enjoys performing poses, consider yoga classes for kids or learn a few more poses together. Now that we have covered some of the most common concurrent conditions or issues that Autistic girls can face, it's time to move to the next chapter on the ins and outs of diagnosis.

: RECEIVING A DIAGNOSIS

 "One reason I've done as well as I have is early intervention—
I was 'got at' very young."

— ROS BLACKBURN (STEWART 2024)

You may be at a point in which you are considering the pros and cons of obtaining an Autism diagnosis for your daughter. In this chapter, we will consider different viewpoints on this subject and highlight the steps involved in the process.

In the introduction to this book, I mentioned that receiving an Autism diagnosis at the age of thirty was no less than a lifeline for me. It helped me understand all the things that made me feel different and "wrong," and enabled me to accept myself. Many Autistic friends have told me that while they did not need specific support, benefits, or understanding to perform the basic tasks of human functioning… they needed all these things to live up to their full potential.

In Chapter One, I mentioned that girls are diagnosed later than boys because of the stereotyping of Autistic traits and because clinicians often rely on male Autistic social skills profiles. Even when girls display the same clinical signs as boys, they are likely to receive a different diagnosis. Those who have lower support needs than males, meanwhile, may appear typical and display similar behaviors to typical boys and their Autism may once again go unnoticed. In her 2015 book *Women and Girls with Autism Spectrum Disorder*, author Sarah Hendrickx points to studies revealing the typical route to diagnosis for female Autism. Typically, girls or women are diagnosed with another disorder, one of which may be social anxiety. Some families may request a diagnosis for a daughter with Autism if another family is diagnosed. During the teen years, a girl's coping capacity may appear to decline, and they may not display typically female interests in topics like clothing, beauty, or relationships. Sometimes, adult women are first diagnosed with schizophrenia or a psychotic disorder before they are diagnosed with Autism.

THE NEED FOR GREATER AWARENESS AMONG CLINICIANS AND OTHER PROFESSIONALS

A 2023 narrative review by Cook et al. has found that biases continue to be prevalent in the diagnostic procedure for Autism, with some girls and women being diagnosed late or missing out completely on a diagnosis. One proposed reason for this bias is the differences in Autism presentation across genders, as discussed above. There are no reliable biomarkers or tests that can conclusively point to Autism.

There are three levels used to measure Autism:

- Broad constructs (core diagnostic criteria such as restricted and limited behaviors)
- Narrow constructs (subdivisions of broad characteristics—for example, repetitive motor actions)
- Behavioral exemplars (specific examples of characteristics such as repeatedly touching certain objects or textures, or rocking back and forth)

Cook and Hull note that the main gender difference exists at the behavioral exemplar level. That is, the characteristics of Autism in boys and girls may be identical or similar, but the specific behaviors expressed by each may be different. Unfortunately, it is these behaviors that are used for current diagnostics.

For instance, within the broad construct of "social interaction," clinicians often look for the behavioral exemplar of a child finding it tough to make friends. Yet research has shown that although Autistic boys may find it hard to establish close friendships, Autistic girls may have many close friends, similar in number to non-Autistic girls. However, they may have higher rates of conflicts with their friends than Autistic boys do. As such, the number of friends a child has is simply not a reliable bar against which to measure the likelihood of Autism in girls. Cook and Hull recommend a broadening of the behavioral exemplars included in the diagnostic process, to capture a wider range of presentations.

They also note that Autistic girls and women have higher levels of masking than boys and men. Some may be so adept at camouflaging that they have to actively stop masking for their Autistic characteristics to be observed by a clinician. Another suggestion is that some Autistic girls can have fewer or less intense Autistic characteristics in early childhood but that these can increase so that by adolescence, their characteristics are more obvious.

Yet another impediment to earlier diagnosis may be concurrent conditions, many of which were mentioned in the previous chapter. The presence of mental conditions, in particular, may overshadow Autism or vice versa. Some conditions occur more frequently in girls and women than in boys and men—including anxiety, which is also high in nonbinary adults. Sometimes, anxiety results from having Autism and being in a poorly adapted environment. As such, traditional treatments that do not take Autism into account may miss their mark. Researchers are therefore pointing to a need to carefully differentiate the characteristics of each, to identify potential differences in how anxiety that co-occurs with Autism is similar or different to anxiety in neurotypical people.

Eating disorders, say Cook and Hull, are yet another reason why Autism is sometimes hard to spot. Up to 30 percent of women being treated for anorexia nervosa are Autistic and in most cases, Autism is not diagnosed until several years after the eating disorder manifests itself. This can have serious consequences for those who are not diagnosed until they are already in recovery from their eating disorder. Recovery may be incomplete or absent if the triggers for eating disorders are related to sensory sensitivities and emotional management, and these issues are not addressed.

The researchers therefore recommend that girls with eating disorders should also be screened for Autism. They concluded that existing guidelines for diagnosis (such as those contained in the DSM-5) do not need to be radically overhauled, but they would benefit from fine-tuning. Cook and Hull created a table of recommendations, which includes a push for greater awareness in clinicians of aspects such as the diagnostic bias against girls (and why this bias exists). They also stated that the accuracy of assessment can be improved by clinicians adopting the following strategies:

- Embracing a multimodal means of assessment (including self-reporting, direct observation, and reports from others).
- Combining assessments for Autism with comprehensive screening for various mental health and other neurodevelopmental issues.
- Using a broad assessment and diagnostic formulation that covers the characteristics of the person and their environment. This would suggest ways to improve their well-being and functioning.
- Being flexible when searching for behavioral exemplars, taking into account the ways in which sex/gender can influence these exemplars.

- Making diagnostic decisions based on quantitative and qualitative information.
- Camouflaging should be assessed using standardized measures such as the Camouflaging of Autistic Traits Questionnaire (CAT-Q). The latter is a self-report measure of social camouflaging behaviors in adults. It can be used to identify Autistic people who do not meet diagnostic criteria because of their ability to mask or camouflage their symptoms.

THE PROS AND CONS OF EARLY DIAGNOSIS

Below are a few important considerations regarding diagnosis.

✚ Pros include (Okoye et al. 2023):

- Being able to access required services
- Reduced stress for the child
- The possibility of accessing targeted interventions and enjoying a better social life and greater independence in one's childhood years and adulthood
- Having help for honing essential skills like social interaction, fine and gross motor skills, strength and movement, communication, thinking and learning, and emotional skills
- Scientific evidence suggests that an early diagnosis leads to significant improvements in cognitive, language, and social-emotional functioning in children
- Less stress and anxiety for parents, who can stop judging themselves for not knowing how to help their daughters
- Better social outcomes and greater independence

━ Cons include:

- Having limitations unintentionally placed on a child by family members and teachers

- Discrimination, bullying, and/or judgment from others once they discover a child's diagnosis
- A risk of overdiagnosis or misdiagnosis, potentially leading to unnecessary treatments
- A reduced chance of being diagnosed for issues like ADHD, even when a child displays symptoms of this disorder
- The emotional challenges of diagnosis (since the process can require comprehensive assessment from multiple teams)

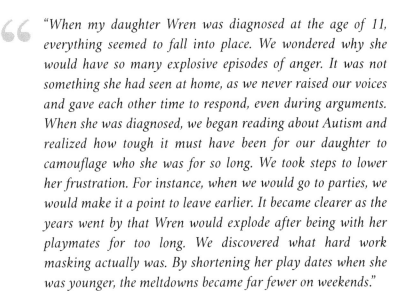

"When my daughter Wren was diagnosed at the age of 11, everything seemed to fall into place. We wondered why she would have so many explosive episodes of anger. It was not something she had seen at home, as we never raised our voices and gave each other time to respond, even during arguments. When she was diagnosed, we began reading about Autism and realized how tough it must have been for our daughter to camouflage who she was for so long. We took steps to lower her frustration. For instance, when we would go to parties, we would make it a point to leave earlier. It became clearer as the years went by that Wren would explode after being with her playmates for too long. We discovered what hard work masking actually was. By shortening her play dates when she was younger, the meltdowns became far fewer on weekends."

— KAI, 42

"Before my daughter, Kyla, was diagnosed, I used to stop her when she would twirl her hair or make repetitive noises. Once we realized that these were stimming behaviors she was using to soothe herself, we refrained from interfering. What made a difference for us was deciding that it wasn't Kyla's job to make everyone else feel comfortable at her own expense. Asking her to stop stimming was like asking someone who was starting not to have a bite of a dish that was placed before them. We explained to Kyla that if someone asked her about

the stimming, she could explain that it made her feel better. We found that most people stopped judging or teasing her when they understood the reasons for her behaviors."

— JACKIE, 51

EARLY SCREENING AND DIAGNOSIS

A diagnosis can be made as early as two years (or even eighteen months) though the average age for girls is four (it is three for boys). The health care professional may use one or more of the following screening tools to determine whether further evaluation is needed (Lovering 2022):

- **Modified Checklist for Autism in Toddlers, Revised (M-CHAT)**

A parent-completed questionnaire used to identify children at risk.

- **The Ages and Stages Questionnaire (ASQ)**

This tool is used to identify developmental delays in kids aged between one and five-and-a-half years old. It comprises a questionnaire filled in by parents that focuses on communication, problem-solving, personal adaptive, and other skills.

- **Screening Tool for Autism in Toddlers and Young Children (STAT)**

An interactive screening tool designed for children, comprising twelve activities assessing skills like play, communication, and imitation skills: takes around twenty minutes to administer.

- **Parents' Evaluation of Developmental Status (PEDS)**

A parent interview form focusing on developmental and behavioral issues.

- **Communication and Behavior Scales (CSBS)**

A test comprising both parent interviews and direct observations of natural play to collect information on communication development.

The American Academy of Pediatrics recommends developmental and behavioral screening and well-child care visits when a child is nine months, eighteen months, and thirty months in age. Screening for ASD is also recommended at eighteen and twenty-four months.

If you and your child's primary care provider feel that your child should be evaluated for ASD, an appointment is made with a trained specialist. Once you have the recommendation from your child's physician and insurance verification for your child, you can schedule this appointment. Prior to meeting the clinician, you will be given a form with various questions about your child's behavioral, medical, socio-emotional, and developmental history. At this stage, it is a good idea to gather your child's school records, Individualized Education Program (IEP) if your child has one, and any other relevant assessments. Take a look back at your child's milestones so you can address any concerns you may have.

The diagnostician will then meet you and conduct a semi-structured interview with you using the Autism Diagnostic Inventory, Revised (ADI-R). They then conduct an assessment, which takes thirty to sixty minutes. You can stay with your child during this assessment if you wish and, if your child is toddler-aged, you may be requested to be present. The parent's main role is to just observe, though the clinician may ask you to interact with your child in specific ways at specific points.

There are different diagnostic tools available, and some insurance companies may request a specific tool to be used. The most commonly used assessment tool is the Autism Diagnostic Observation Schedule, Second Edition (ADOS-2), which is considered the "gold standard" tool. It is an activity-based means of evaluating communication skills, social interaction, and the imaginative use of materials in people who are suspected to have ASD (Dreison n.d.).

After the evaluation, the clinician will discuss the results with you. This may occur during the same appointment or at a follow-up meeting. The clinician will also provide you with a written report with useful recommendations and let you know which interventions they believe are most likely to aid in your child's development. This is usually sent to you one to two weeks after the assessment (Autism Learning Partners n.d.).

JOURNALING ACTIVITY

If you're considering having your child assessed, take your journal and answer the following questions, which will help you clarify whether you feel obtaining a diagnosis is the right choice for your family:

1. What behaviors in my daughter have I noticed that lead me to think she could be on the spectrum?
2. How have these behaviors differed across different settings and situations?
3. How do these behaviors impact my child's social life/emotional well-being/learning progress?
4. Have I discussed my concerns with my child's teachers or caregivers?
5. Am I prepared for the implications that a diagnosis could have on my family dynamics?
6. Am I prepared to support my daughter with the challenges or stigma that can accompany a diagnosis of Autism?

7. What role do I envision for myself and other family members to support our daughter?

Now that you have weighed up the pros and cons of having a diagnosis, we will turn to one of the most important aspects of parenting an Autistic girl: understanding and respecting her sensory needs.

L: LENDING SENSORY SUPPORT

UNDERSTANDING AND RESPECTING YOUR CHILD'S SENSORY NEEDS

"When a family focuses on ability instead of disability, all things are possible."

— STUART DUNCAN (CIRCLE CARE SERVICES, N.D.)

Like many other Autistic girls, sensory issues abounded in my childhood and youth. In my early childhood, the daycare I went to provided freshly cut fruit platters for our morning break, and I couldn't bear to eat any. To this day, I find the texture of fruit completely disgusting. At mid-morning and mid-afternoon, I'd rather go hungry and wait until my next main meal than eat fruit. Another big issue for me is wet wrists. I can't stand my wrists being wet if the rest of my body is dry. Even thinking about it makes me cringe! This goes to the extent that I would rather throw out dishes than wash them. I am a good dryer and I find stacking dishes in the dishwasher a breeze… but washing will never be a task I am comfortable carrying out.

I am very particular about the textures that surround me. When my wife and I purchased our home, we decided to re-carpet the floors before moving in. We went to a carpet store and I had to touch every single one of their carpet choices. I didn't want the salesperson or my wife to talk to me so I could focus on the mission at hand (pun not intended). I went through the store at a rather manic pace, touching the carpets to find the softest one. I did! The carpet is deliciously soft!

One habit I embrace rigorously is that of "washing the outside world off." Every time I leave our home, when I return, I take a shower right away to help me calm down from the sensory overload. As was the case in my youth, I still have a big interest in physical activity. Weights, bike riding, and running are activities that I do almost every day. I don't do so for fitness reasons, but rather, because my brain and energy levels go through such high activity levels that I need to be a little worn out to function on a balanced level. All these activities are like a lifeline to me. I would be terribly distressed if I could not choose these means of calming myself and obtaining better focus.

THE AUTISTIC BRAIN AND SENSORY ISSUES

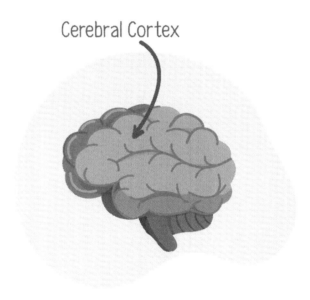

Cerebral Cortex

Over the past couple of decades, neuroimaging studies have revealed the underlying neurobiological mechanisms of ASD. One UCLA-led study showed that brain changes are prevalent throughout the cerebral cortex—the outermost layer that surrounds the brain—in people with ASD. The cerebral cortex comprises gray matter and it is filled with billions of neurons used to conduct high-level executive functions. These are the set of higher-order cognitive abilities that enable us to understand complex or abstract concepts, solve new problems, plan an event, and manage our relationships.

In the study, the scientists examined gene expression in eleven cortical regions by sequencing RNA from the four main cortical lobes in the brain. They discovered significant changes in nearly all the eleven cortical regions, including those involved in reasoning, language, social cognition, mental flexibility, and the primary sensory regions. They found that the largest changes in RNA levels were found in the visual cortex and the parietal cortex—which process information like pain, touch, and temperature. The researchers stated that this may reflect the sensory hypersensitivity that Autistic people typically have (UCLA Health 2022).

One previous study (Guo et al. 2019) found that in the Autistic brain, differences exist in the development of the anterior cingulate cortex (a part of the brain involved with decision-making, impulse control, emotional regulation, and attention). Autistic people also have delayed, reduced development of specific neurons (VENS neurons), which help human beings rapidly and intuitively process complex situations. As such, they can struggle with novel situations.

Despite the big progress that has been made in the understanding of brain differences among Autistic people, much still remains a mystery. One of the leading biological theories of Autism, which is supported by numerous studies, is a model of cortical hyperexcitability. That is, our neurons are easily activated and do not discriminate as efficiently between phenomena we wish to ignore and important situations taking place that merit our attention.

One recent study published in the journal *Molecular Autism* showed that the brain stem (located in the lower, back half of the brain) may play a vital role in the elevated sensory responses of Autistic children. Its location makes sense when you consider that sensory information comes from the body through the spinal cord to the brain stem, and then the rest of the brain. In the study, the parents or caregivers of sixty-one Autistic and seventy-two non-Autistic children (with an average age of eight years old) were given a report to complete regarding their children's hyperresponsiveness (increased sensitivity to stimuli) or hyporesponsiveness (reduced sensitivity to stimuli). The children then underwent magnetic resonance imaging (MRI) to obtain brain images (Rivera-Bonet 2023).

The researchers, headed by Dr. Brittany G. Travers, wished to focus on connectivity within the brain stem, so they investigated the "white matter tract" microstructure. The latter enables communication between different parts of the brain by serving as connecting fibers between them. The structure of white matter tracts in the brain stem was found to be related to sensory responses in Autistic kids, while playing a different role in those of non-Autistic kids. The most significant relationship with brain stem white matter was found for two sensory aspects: touch and hyporesponsiveness. The scientists also found that most sensory-brain relationships occurred in the brain stem and cerebellum. The findings revealed that alterations of sensory responses in Autism may be directed by white matter in the brain stem—an area that is involved in reflex-like behaviors rather than conscious control. The scientists concluded that all this information shows that interventions that ask Autistic children to control their sensory responses are futile because these responses seem to be extremely reflexive (or beyond one's control).

An even more recent study by Dr. Travers showed that there are two specific nuclei in the brain stem that explain differences in Autistic people. The first is involved in the pain processing system for internal organs and it shows a significant relationship with increased repetitive behaviors. The second is involved in digestion, swallowing, eating, and cardio-respiration and it is linked to communication challenges. Dr. Travers hypothesizes that these structural differences can contribute to the gastrointestinal issues and trouble with eating or swallowing that so many Autistic people can have (Leclerc 2024).

Additional research explaining how the Autistic brain differs was carried out as far back as 2013 by Stanford University School of Medicine researchers. They found that there is a remarkably high level of hyperconnectivity in the brains of Autistic kids. However, some networks are underconnected. They also found that the degree of hyperconnectivity in the brain predicted the severity of restricted and repetitive behaviors such as intense focus on one object or interest. The researchers hypothesized that some types of external stimuli may be unable to engage the Autistic brain's attentional system. As a result, a child may become deeply engrossed in a narrow range of behaviors instead of adapting to external stimuli (Digitale 2013).

Findings such as these can explain why kids with Autism can become analytical and home in on small details instead of the big picture. At times, they can be hyperreactive to even the tiniest sensorial stimuli, yet they may seem oblivious to others. They can also explain why processing situations can be so much more energy- and time-consuming for Autistic people.

SENSORY SYSTEMS AT PLAY

We know that sensory integration can be more challenging for Autistic girls and boys. Knowing about their brain differences, it is easy to see how processing so many senses can be a big challenge for them. When talking about senses, you may usually think of the Big Five—sight, hearing, smell, taste, and touch. Aristotle (384–322BC) is credited with first numbering the senses in his written work, *De Anima*. However, neurologists have identified as many as twenty-one senses! They include:

- **Equilibrioception:** The perception of balance.
- **Proprioception:** In Chapter Two, we introduced the sense of proprioception, which essentially amounts to body awareness (for instance, being able to close your eyes and touch your ear) and being aware of where your body is in space.
- **Nociception:** The detection of painful stimuli.
- **Thermoception:** The sense that enables us to perceive heat.
- **Interoception:** The process of sensing signals from the body such as those indicating we are hungry, our heart is beating, we need to go to the bathroom, and similar.
- **The vestibular sense:** Also known as the movement, balance, or gravity sense, the vestibular sense enables us to move smoothly and maintain our balance while we are moving.

It is easy to see how having to process information from so many senses can be overwhelming for us. When any one of these senses is misaligned, it can transform a day, or a moment, from wonderful to unbearable.

TIPS FOR REDUCING STRESS AND ANXIETY FOR YOUR DAUGHTER

Let's take a look at how some of our senses can be impacted by Autism (Autism Together n.d.).

The Sense of Sight

Autism can overwhelm or underwhelm the senses, meaning that a child may see objects as brighter or darker than a neurotypical child might. Sometimes, objects may appear to jump around or become fragmented. A child with an under-responsive sense of sight might be attracted to experiences that boost the visual input they are receiving. They might be drawn to tiny details that others seem to ignore or start at sources of light or patterns of color. Someone with oversensitive sight, on the other hand, might find it difficult to maintain eye contact.

Sensory Tip: If your child is under-responsive, they might benefit from having a night light or playing with toys that have light features. If they are oversensitive to visual stimuli, then dimming lights and reducing eye contact may be soothing to them.

The Sense of Touch

Autistic kids can also vary greatly in how they use touch to make sense of the world. Touch seekers may seek out different textures and they may have a high pain threshold, sometimes injuring themselves or chewing on inedible items. Those who are averse to touch may find being touched unpleasant, uncomfortable, or downright painful. They may also have a narrow number of clothing textures they feel comfortable wearing.

Sensory Tip: If your child loves touching things, prioritize texture when buying them clothes, reading materials, and toys. If they are particular about clothing, take note of the type of materials they are most comfortable with and consider buying them seamless, soft items that do not have constrictive buttons, belts, and other items that can distress them.

The Sense of Hearing

Autistic kids can have numerous difficulties with respect to sound. For instance, they can find it hard to filter and process sounds. They may be oversensitive to sound and find particular sounds (including sirens, babies crying, or dogs barking) unbearable. If they are under-sensitive to sound, then they may raise the volume very high when they are listening to music or benefit from communicating in louder volumes.

Some Autistic kids have auditory agnosia—which makes it difficult to hear or interpret sounds despite having typical hearing function. For instance, they may hear the school bell ring but need to be reminded that the class is over. Kids with this neurological condition may hear things perfectly but struggle to make sense of them. Finally, Autistic kids with tonal agnosia may find it hard to understand the tone or inflection others are using.

Sensory Tip: To help a child with agnosia, be clear and concise and repeat information that your child may not have grasped the first time around.

The Sense of Smell

Kids with a hypersensitive sense of smell may be overwhelmed by specific smells—including perfumes, foods, beauty products, or car fuel. If they are under-responsive, they may be drawn to strong smells like essential oils, perfumes, and spices.

Sensory Tip: Keep your home fragrance-free if your child is oversensitive to smells. If they are attracted to smells, on the other hand, delight them with an essential oil diffuser, perfume, and fragrant dishes.

The Sense of Taste

Autistic children may prefer foods that are sweet, sour, bitter, or salty. Some may find some tastes and flavors too strong, and others may enjoy very spicy foods. Those with an under-responsive sense of taste may even eat non-edible items.

Sensory Tip: Aim to introduce new foods to your diet by slowly introducing them to foods that have a similar texture or taste to the food they like.

Vestibular (Balance)

The vestibular system is contained in your inner ears. It helps you control and balance your body. Kids with an oversensitive vestibular system may have motion sickness. Those with an under-responsive system may seek out activities that enable them to move their bodies. They may appear hyperactive and enjoy activities like gymnastics, going on fairground rides, swimming, and similar

Sensory Tip: If your child's vestibular system is overstimulated, repetitive movements like rocking or swinging may calm their system through movement, as may yoga poses. If your child enjoys movement, then give her access to a myriad of activities, exercises, and days out.

Proprioception (Body Awareness)

As mentioned above, proprioception enables us to work out where our body is in relation to things. In open spaces, it makes us aware of how our bodies are moving. Messages sent from our muscles and joints tell our brains where we are. They also allow us to regulate how we move, our posture, and how much pressure we need to use to do things. For instance, when we are baking a cake and we need to measure the flour we are using, we know to run the knife very gently along the cup to obtain an exact measurement. If we do so too quickly, then flour can get all over the place. If a child is oversensitive, they may seem awkward or clumsy, and they may frequently drop items, trip, or knock things over. They may unintentionally break things like a pencil or book and may feel very bad about doing so. If they are under-responsive, they may seek more sensory stimulation by banging things, stomping on the ground, biting their fingers, and similar.

Sensory Tip: Talk to an occupational therapist about sensory tools like weighted backpacks, which can help give a child sensory feedback when they are out and about.

An occupational therapist can help you understand the specific challenges your child may be facing, helping you detect when senses are over or under-responsive. Some senses can vary greatly, and it pays to adapt the strategies you use to help your child.

> *"I had a few things I couldn't stand when I was at school, including socks with seams, shirts with tags, and tight hair clips or ties. I couldn't stand lumpy foods either, like yogurt with fruity bits and lumpy oatmeal. If it were up to me I would live on milkshakes."*
>
> — CARMEN, 32

> *"We created a routine to help our daughter relax after her busy day at school. We always had one of her favorite snacks ready in the car and when we got home, we kept things quiet (no TV, no music) for around an hour. If she had a meltdown we would invite her to calm down in her quiet place. We started doing a bit of meditation when she was around eight and she used to ask for a session once she got used to it... it became part of her bedtime routine."*
>
> — CHARLIE, 53

STIMMING

Stimming, which is short for self-stimulation, is a technique that can help Autistic people manage overwhelming emotions and deal with difficult or stressful situations. Stimming can involve:

- Fiddling with the hands and fingers or with objects such as erasers, pencils, or paper
- Repetitive body movements like rocking, banging the head, or swinging
- Seeking visual stimulation

- Chewing items or one's fingers or nails
- Listening to the same music or sound over and over
- Scratching or rubbing the skin
- Flapping the arms
- Twirling
- Smelling or sniffing things
- Bouncing
- Tapping things or objects repeatedly
- Flicking the fingers
- Hand flapping

The triggers that may lead your child to stim can vary. They can range from being physically uncomfortable to experiencing sensory overload, strong emotions, or boredom. Some children are triggered by objects, activities, or sensations they enjoy immensely. They may use stimming to engage with these things or experiences.

There is no reason to stop your daughter from stimming if it is not causing her or others harm, or if it is not dangerous. There are many ways to manage stimming, including occupational therapy and adjusting your child's environment to reduce stress. An occupational therapist can help you create a bespoke "sensory diet" for your daughter. The latter involves scheduling activities into your child's day to meet their sensory demands. You can also implement environmental changes (such as placing your child in a smaller class or school) and give your child stress management tools (such as a stress ball or fidget spinner).

SENSORY THERAPY

An occupational therapist can play a pivotal role in reducing the stress that sensory issues can cause your child. They can assess overresponsiveness or underresponsiveness to the different senses, and share useful techniques to help quell their discomfort and pain. They will also be able to give you vital information regarding how your child's sensory needs change throughout the day, which senses are stronger than others, and what triggers you can aim to reduce or eliminate from your child's life (Notbohm 2019).

 "My daughter, Noa, never wanted to miss out when one of her friends threw a party. However, not ten minutes into a party, she would become overwhelmed by the sound of music, people chatting, and plates and cutlery being placed on a table. Her occupational therapist suggested using noise-canceling headphones and we got her some in-ear headphones. She told her friends about them before the next party, so everyone knew she would be wearing them at the next party. The very first time she wore them, she stayed much longer than at previous parties and felt less anxious the next time she was invited to one."

— NEIL, 47

THE AUTISTIC AND ADHD NERVOUS SYSTEM

Autistic and ADHD kids can frequently experience hyperarousal or hypoarousal owing to their vulnerable nervous systems. In Chapter Two, we saw how we can have higher rates of stress, anxiety, depression, and stress. We can also find it harder to adapt to unexpected changes. As explained by Dr. Megan Anna Neff (2023), a neurodivergent psychologist with Autism and ADHD, the human nervous system comprises both the central nervous system (the CNS, comprising the brain and spinal cord) and the peripheral nervous system (PNS). The PNS is made up of nerves, neurons, and ganglia lying outside the brain and spinal cord and throughout the body. The CNS, meanwhile, is our major control center.

The PNS is divided into the somatic nervous system (which is responsible for voluntary movement) and the autonomic nervous system (or ANS, which controls movements that are not within our conscious control, including our breathing). When discussing stress, anxiety, and overwhelm, the autonomic nervous system is the main player.

THE AUTONOMIC NERVOUS SYSTEM

The ANS is made up of the sympathetic and parasympathetic nervous systems. The sympathetic nervous system is responsible for activating your body—for instance, causing your heart and breathing rates to rise. When the sympathetic system is stimulated, we can go into "fight or flight" mode. That is, our heart rate increases, our muscles grow tense, we begin to take more rapid, shallow breaths, our focus narrows, our digestive system slows, and our immune system functions poorly. The parasympathetic system, on the other hand, allows your body's systems to slow and calm down. It allows our heart rate to decrease and our digestive system to digest our food. It enables our immune system to fight off disease and allows us to take deep breaths. The part of the brain that balances these two systems is the hypothalamus.

THE VAGUS NERVE

Another crucial component of our nervous system is the vagus nerve. It is the largest cranial nerve belonging to the parasympathetic system and it comprises two sides: the ventral vagal system (on the front) and the dorsal vagal system (on the back). Let's begin with the ventral vagal system. When activated, it helps the sympathetic and parasympathetic systems work in harmony. When we are under extreme stress, on the other hand, the dorsal vagus nerves take command. It protects us from experiencing pain and trauma by shutting our systems down, causing us to feel numb or distancing us from the source of our stress.

To battle stress, it helps to enhance our vagal tone, since when we have a high vagal tone, our ventral vagal system (which helps us recover from stressful events more quickly) is running the show.

When we have low vagal tone, on the other hand, it means that we are less able to deal with stress, we find changes harder to adapt to, and our window of stress tolerance narrows down. This leaves us more vulnerable to hyperarousal or hypoarousal. In a state of hyperarousal, we can feel anxious, hypervigilant, and nervous. When we are hypoaroused, we shut down, and sensations like fatigue, numbness, or depression can take over.

HOW TO BOOST YOUR CHILD'S VAGAL TONE

There are many gentle ways to reset your nervous system and enhance your child's vagal tone. These include some of the approaches I mentioned earlier, including breathwork, exercise, mindfulness meditation, and consuming gut-friendly foods. Studies have also shown that the following activities can boost vagal tone: humming, chanting, singing, massage, and relaxation exercises such as progressive muscle relaxation, which simply involves tensing and relaxing the different muscles in the body to enter into a state of relaxation. One study showed, for instance, that "Om" chanting creates a sensation of vibration that stimulates the vagus nerve (Kalyani et al. 2011).

Fun Fact: If you want to measure your daughter's vagal tone, one good way to do so is by measuring her heart rate variability (HRV)—the variation in the time interval between heartbeats. Your HRV is a direct measure of the dynamic interplay between your sympathetic and parasympathetic systems. Having a high HRV is linked to better autonomic nervous system function and enhanced adaptability to stressors. There are many everyday, affordable devices you can use to measure your HRV—including heart rate sensors and some smart-watches.

TECHNIQUES TO HELP MANAGE SENSORY OVERLOAD

There are many more additional techniques that may work well with your daughter, which is why having an open mindset and a willingness to try out many techniques is important (Williams 2020). My Autistic friends and I often chat about how we calm down when things get a bit overwhelming. The following is a list we have compiled together. We are hopeful that others may find one or more techniques as useful as we do.

The Rule of One

When a child is in distress, the tendency can be for various people to rush in to help them. When a child is hyperaroused, however, having so many people talking to them at once can only make things worse. Instead, follow the rule of one. One person should approach her and suggest just one activity to make her feel better—for instance, a few deep breathing exercises or going to her calm place.

Isometric Exercise

I mentioned progressive muscle relaxation earlier and the relaxing effect that tightening and releasing your muscles can have. Your child doesn't have to be lying down and they don't have to squeeze all their muscles to curb stress, however. They can simply perform an isometric exercise like pushing their knees together, pushing against a wall, or pulling a rope tied to a sturdy surface. When they release the tension, they will notice how much more relaxed their muscles feel.

Deep Pressure

Similarly to isometric exercises, deep pressure can help a child with Autism calm down. Deep pressure can be applied via a weighted blanket, compression vest, compression swing, weighted stuffed toy, or even with a bear hug (but only if your child wants one). Play Dough or

Crazy Aaron's Thinking Putty (a silicone-based putty that is safe and never dries out) are great choices. The latter comes with appealing elements such as glitter and confetti.

A Box of Fun

Have a box filled with tactile items your daughter can squeeze, touch, and play with when things get a little stressful. It can include foam cubes, textured bangle bracelets, weighted sensory knot balls, stretchy putty, digit items, and more.

A Ball Pit

If your daughter loves playing in ball pits, then having a small one of their own at home can be a huge source of fun and relief. These pits can be filled with foam cubes and soft balls, which your daughter may enjoy jumping on. When I see all the toys that are available online now, I always think I wish I had had these when I was a kid.

A Quiet Space

If your child needs silence to wind down, ensure they have a space in the home that they can call their own—if possible, make it sound-proof. You can also use sound-blocking headphones, which work well to drown out environmental noise.

Let your daughter's teachers and occupational therapist (if they have an OT) know which sensory techniques work for her. Teachers who know how to calm down an Autistic child and who have access to tools that work can make a big difference by reducing the stress your daughter may face at school or in a therapeutic setting.

MINDFULNESS ACTIVITIES

It's now time to end the chapter with mindfulness activities that can teach your child the value of simply being in the present moment. We have already been through breathing and yoga. Try the following activities to add a bit of variety to the equation:

- **Mindful Coloring**

Mindful coloring books contain mindfulness-inspired illustrations with lots of small and larger spaces to draw. Encourage your child to concentrate on her coloring and the shapes that pop to life as she works on them. The aim is to enhance focus and empower the mind to view thoughts and emotions in an open, non-judgmental way.

- **Mindful Walking**

A trend that started in Japan and is taking the world by storm is that of "shinrin yoku," or forest bathing. It involves heading to a forest and opening the senses to the world around you. Encourage your child to listen to the birdsong and the sounds of leaves rustling. Ask her to touch different textures such as tree bark, leaves, and flowers. Take a few drawing materials along and draw a flower, and smell the freshness of the leaves and trees. You don't need to live near a forest to engage in this activity. A park, beach, or other natural area will also do.

- **Mindful Storytelling**

Create a story together, and record or write it down. Revisit the story every evening before your child goes to bed and add details to each scene.

- **Making a Glitter Jar**

Take a half-pint-sized transparent jar. Add around two tablespoons of small glitter and one teaspoon of large glitter (or small items like snowflakes, stars, and other slightly larger pieces) to the bottom of the jar. Fill it with hot (but not boiling) water and leave around a half-inch of headspace. Add around three tablespoons of glitter glue to the water. Place a bead or two of superglue on the lip of the jar and close it tightly. Shake the jar until the glitter glue dissolves. Invite your daughter to shake this jar and watch all the glitter settle when she feels stressed.

- **A Guided Mindfulness Script**

Play some relaxing music and ask your daughter to lie or sit in a comfortable spot while you read the following script, guiding your daughter in a bespoke meditation session. Change the details of the script following your daughter's interests.

1. Let's start by checking in with our bodies. How do you feel now? Can you feel your feet on the ground or your body on the chair? Is there any part of your body that feels tight? If so, squeeze it, then let go and relax.
2. Now it's time for some breathing. Breathe in to the count of four (count to four for your child). Hold your breath to the count of four. Breathe out to the count of four. Pause to the count of four (Repeat this exercise a few times).
3. Now imagine that you are high up on a cloud. You are light as a feather and the cloud is moving slowly from one side of the sky to the other. The sky is blue and it is sunny, and you feel peaceful as you move along.
4. Now, as I count from one to five, you start to feel heavier... (count from one to five and say "heavier" after every number). Now you are nestled deep within the cloud, and it embraces

you and feels soft and cuddly. You are enjoying your ride and feeling more and more relaxed.

5. Wiggle your toes a bit and notice how they feel. Next, notice your legs, your tummy, your hands, your arms, your neck, and your head… notice how relaxed each part of your body is.

6. Stay in your cloud for as long as you like and when you are ready, float gently down to a soft, lush forest. There, I will be waiting for you, ready to give you a hug.

In this chapter, we have immersed ourselves in the whys and where-fores of the sensory world. In the next chapter, we will focus on your child's learning experience and how to ensure it is positive, vibrant, and adapted to their needs.

S: SUPPORTING YOUR CHILD'S LEARNING JOURNEY

STRATEGIES FOR HELPING YOUR CHILD IN ACADEMIC PURSUITS

> *"If they can't learn the way we teach, we teach the way they learn."*

— DR. O. IVAR LOVAAS (CIRCLE CARE SERVICES, N.D.)

School is one of a child's most vital life experiences but, for Autistic kids, it can also be one of the most challenging. My school years were filled with ups and downs. I was an excellent runner and I hyperfixated on it and was really into training, diet, and recovery. I was a track and field athlete and I also competed at a state level in cross-country. If sport was my savior, school was my biggest bugbear. I struggled academically, particularly when it came to understanding my teachers. I simply couldn't work out what they were saying or follow their method of teaching.

I remember that for my senior year art assessment, we were asked to create a self-portrait. I thought it was ridiculous to portray my physical appearance because that was just the packaging, not the essence. So I attempted to paint my soul. I failed the assessment. To this day, I get compliments on how beautiful the painting is. I knew I was going to fail, but my sense of logic was stronger than my need to pass.

I would often take things quite literally, or zone in on small details and not pay too much attention to the big picture. For instance, at university, I had to select my semester units for the following year. I chose a subject that I hadn't done before. When I spoke to my course coordinator the following year, she asked me why I repeated a subject I had already passed I asked her what she meant, and the two units I had completed were identical; only the name had changed. Side note: I didn't notice at all and got the same grades twice!

WHY AUTISTIC GIRLS CAN STRUGGLE WITH LEARNING

Autistic girls can have many specific issues, including:

- **Struggles with Social Skills**

ASD can make it harder to understand and respond to social cues. Social skills become more important at school as kids get older, as they are crucial for participating in group projects, showing teamwork, and building positive relationships with teachers.

One area that can be a big struggle is the use of social language (particularly figurative language or the ability to understand more than what is explicitly stated). Autistic people can interpret words literally when they are meant ironically or sarcastically. They may also home in on the literal meaning of metaphors instead of seeing them as symbols. This can make it harder to establish relationships with their peers and teachers.

- **Difficulties Processing Information**

Autistic students may find it difficult to understand and recall information shared in class. They may struggle with organizing their thoughts, planning tasks, and completing tasks on time, all of which can make them feel like they can never keep up with their classmates' pace.

They may additionally struggle with sharing their thoughts in group discussions for two reasons: it can be hard to organize their thoughts and they may feel overstimulated when people talk over each other.

- **Reading and Verbal Comprehension**

Autistic children usually do as well as or better than their peers at decoding written words. However, they are more skilled at sounding or identifying words than understanding what they have read. This may be because decoding is more abstract, while comprehension is more concrete. It requires the reader to be aware of the story structure, pick up on references, and make inferences using previous knowledge. Verbal expression and comprehension can also be more difficult because of problems understanding figurative or expressive language.

- **Executive Functioning**

The ability to plan and carry out multistep tasks while taking task parameters, timelines, and other factors into account is called executive functioning. Executive functioning is required to carry out tasks like homework completion, studying for tests, planning for events, completing school projects, and switching between tasks and topics. It also covers the working memory, flexible thinking, and self-control.

Research shows that working memory can be impaired in Autistic people. This means that when the teacher rattles off a set of instructions, or when there are various instructions to read on a test, the Autistic child may find it harder to remember and apply them.

- **Fine and Gross Motor Skills**

Kids need fine motor skills for tasks like writing, cutting, drawing, and pasting. Gross motor skills are those required for lager movements such as jumping, throwing, or running. Autistic kids typically have both fine and gross motor skill issues, which affects their ability to carry out classwork and sporting activities.

- **Sensory Processing**

We have delved into sensory processing and Autism in Chapter Four. It is easy to see how many of the issues we discussed (including being hypersensitive or hyposensitive) can make it harder to learn. For instance, an Autistic child who is hypersensitive may find the bright lighting, sounds, and layout of a classroom so intrusive that it is impossible to process information such as their teacher's instructions.

- **Communication**

Some Autistic kids have very good communication skills, while others may find it harder to interact with people. For instance, an Autistic child might utilize non-verbal communication (such as taking someone's hand and pushing it toward what they want) instead of asking for something, or they might hand someone an object to communicate. In terms of verbal communication, they may confuse pronouns, utilize echolalia, or make up words, all of which can make communication tougher with others.

- **Changing Rules and Expectations and Changes to Routines**

Routines can be a lifeline for Autistic kids, as can clear rules and expectations. In a school setting, however, changes take place all the time. Kids learn a host of new tasks and activities, and the way they are carried out can change frequently. This can add an element of anxiety and stress to the learning experience. Kids with sensory activities can find it even harder to cope, as new situations can expose them to a wide array of sensory triggers.

- **A Lack of Acceptance or Adaptation to Their Needs**

It has become all too common for Autistic children to leave a school setting, despite wanting and needing an education, because of a lack of acceptance, understanding, and flexibility. Autism acceptance must be taught at schools. Children can benefit greatly from knowing the challenges faced by their Autistic peers, but this can only occur with a concerted effort to debunk myths and present updated information. Educators, too, should have Autism awareness training so that Autistic kids see them as people they can trust and count on.

Despite the significant number of children in the US who are diagnosed with Autism, most general education teachers have insufficient Autism-related instruction. Many teacher education programs stipulate just one overview class covering students with disabilities. Training on the job, meanwhile, is nearly non-existent and rarely obligatory. This means that even the best teachers can be at a loss as to how to support their Autistic pupils (Autism Speaks n.d.).

Teachers can make an enormous difference in their students' lives. When they are aware of their Autistic students' needs, they can take steps such as: reducing excess noise; turning off bright lights; limiting the use of colognes and sprays; following a routine; reconsidering grading requirements that reward or punish depending on traditional participation; considering multimedia tools to provide the class with options to participate other than speaking; giving Autistic students equitable, defined tasks within a group; teaching other students about inclusion; being watchful for bullying; and more. They should also communicate with parents if they are concerned that an undiagnosed student is struggling because of Autism.

- **Anxiety**

When an Autistic child is battling anxiety, it can make it much harder to enjoy learning and engaging with the subjects they are learning. When anxiety is severe, it can stop kids from even wanting to go to school. When they feel anxious, kids can act up more, have more meltdowns, and have sleeping issues. Parents and teachers can help prepare kids for change through visual tools and social stories, and they can share powerful strategies for quelling anxiety, including breathing and muscle relaxation exercises. Parents and teachers can also work together by agreeing to allow a child to feel anxious, without forcing them to "calm down" or "stop worrying" about something. They can also share vital information with each other, including a child's anxiety triggers. Schools can help reduce anxiety by filling in the cognitive issues that arise from living in a non-Autistic world. The problem is not the Autistic child but rather, the rigid, unaccepting, environment they are often forced to live in (Hendrickx 2018).

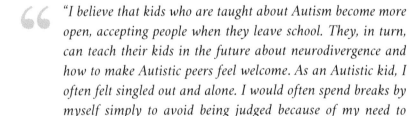

"I believe that kids who are taught about Autism become more open, accepting people when they leave school. They, in turn, can teach their kids in the future about neurodivergence and how to make Autistic peers feel welcome. As an Autistic kid, I often felt singled out and alone. I would often spend breaks by myself simply to avoid being judged because of my need to self-soothe."

— SANI, 42

"I struggled a lot when I started at a new school at the age of eleven. I spent every day alone at lunch and would simply walk around the school, just waiting for the break to finish. I had a teacher who knew I liked to read Percy Jackson books and other books about mythological characters. She started a break time reading club and invited me to join. I didn't find

out until my dad told me, when I was already an adult, that she had started that club because it was centered on my special interest. She was worried that I was alone all the time. I will always be grateful to her."

— MINA, 23

HOW AUTISTIC GIRLS LEARN

Autism is a spectrum disorder, meaning each child has unique learning strengths and challenges. Research shows, however, that many Autistic children are visual thinkers (Rudy 2023). That is, they learn best through images, diagrams, and visual aids. They find it easier to remember things they have just seen than those they have just read about, and they may enjoy drawing, painting, and/or designing. They may find it more enjoyable to learn by using visual apps. To help your child organize her world better, consider using tools like visual schedules, social stories, and visual timers (such as hourglasses) to help them keep track of time.

Fun Fact: The idea that many Autistic learners are visual arose from the writings of Autistic engineer and writer, Temple Grandin. In her book, *Thinking in Pictures* (2006) she explained how she "thinks in pictures" instead of words. This can make skills like conversation more difficult, but it is a big advantage in her profession.

Autistic people can excel at tasks like puzzle making, organizing items, and remembering routes. What's more, because they can have difficulty with spoken and non-verbal communication, they can use visual tools as a means of communicating with others. I wrote earlier that Autistic people can be quite literal in our thinking. This means that abstract concepts like "over," "on the right," or "next month" can be difficult to understand. Using visuals can make all these ideas more graspable. Visual tools are also very important when it comes to teaching your child social intricacies. She may not be able to learn by example because most Autistic people find it hard to read and imitate others. Social stories make things clearer through the use of imagery.

If your child has an auditory learning style, they may prefer to read things out loud, talk about things, and use sound apps and resources. If they have a kinesthetic style, meanwhile, they may benefit from games and activity-based learning. They may need frequent breaks to move around. Kids don't always favor just one learning style. That is, they may learn better by using mind maps but also by listening to music when they are learning. The key to working out your daughter's style is observation.

Knowing your child's learning style is vital because doing so will enable you to help her succeed both at school and in extracurricular activities. It will also boost her confidence and motivate her to take on more challenging tasks. Feeling really good at something is so important for people of all ages. This is because we so often identify strongly with the areas or activities where our strengths shine.

CONCRETE LEARNING

To teach your child new concepts, use concrete language. For instance, if you wish to encourage your child to adopt social behaviors when they meet someone new, teach them "if-then" rules, such as "If someone says hello, say, 'Hello, how are you?'" "If someone says 'Thank you,' say, 'You're welcome.'" Instead of saying "far" or "close" to your child, give concrete measurements, such as "about an arm away." Rather than "Don't run," use "Walk." This is because if you say "Don't run," they may only process "Run," and what you have said may fall flat. Provide your daughter with written lists of the topics you will be covering so there are no surprises. Avoid using unnecessary language that will only interfere with your meaning.

Autistic learners often home in on individual facts or details, then work out the whole picture—though, once again, each child learns differently and some may look at the big picture before specifics.

"Based on my own learning, I think that Autistic people have more detailed thoughts, which means we need more time to get the full picture. But once we do, our level of accuracy is often higher."

— JONAH, 32

"I don't think most of us are 'big picture' learners. I learn in patterns. For instance, in computer science classes, I typically find shortcuts that are only possible if you do see the big picture. I'm drawn to algebraic general solutions because they involve getting the big picture that unites specific classes of problems. In class, my teachers tell me I'm really good at making connections with things, which shows abstract thinking abilities."

— NOLA, 18

HYPERFIXATION AND SPECIAL INTERESTS

In Chapter Seven, we will immerse ourselves more deeply in the topic of special interests but, for now, it is important to mention it in the context of learning—because encouraging your child to home in on their special interests can be a lifesaver for them.

It is helpful to differentiate hyperfixation from hyperfocus. Hyperfixation is a clinical term that describes an intense focus on a specific subject, thing, or person to the point that others are often ignored. When an Autistic child is hyperfixated on something, it can seem like everything else disappears. Both Autistic kids and those with ADHD can hyperfixate on things, especially in their areas of special interest. Hyperfocus is similar in that it also involves being ultra-absorbed in an activity, to the point one may lose interest in other things that are happening at the same time. However, it does not necessarily involve your child's area of interest.

Hyperfixation can be very productive when kids are learning because it allows them to fully engage in a task and stay focused for an extended period. As such, they can achieve more personal and learning goals.

 "I have several subjects I know almost everything there is to know about and I've jumped into many rabbit holes of research. I'm currently doing a Master's in Psychology and these areas of research are hugely useful. It gives me a wider backdrop against which to understand the new information I come across."

— ALIYAH, 27

To help your daughter find her special interests, introduce her to various activities, resources, ideas, and subjects. Take her out to eat and take her shopping, traveling, and to musical concerts—anything you think she might love. When doing so, having a flexible attitude is key. They may not be into something you thought they would be passionate about, and that's okay! You can leave, do something you know they like, and try again with something completely new another day. Don't give up on activities, either! Your child may not be into something this year, but develop an interest in it further down the line. In many ways, introducing special interests to your daughter is similar to introducing them to new foods. The wider the range of items they try, the better. And don't be surprised if your child discovers special interests in their own way.

"I often say that my special interest found me, not the other way around. And in my case, it happened when I was 54. I am a teaching assistant and was helping a PE teacher set up equipment for kinder students. One of these items was a scooter. When I was younger, I could never go on these because I would fall a lot. At 54, my balance was thankfully much better and I found these to be so much fun. I bought an

electric scooter last year and have not stopped since. I go everywhere I can on it and have discovered how to clean, maintain, and repair them. I have joined a scooter group and we meet regularly to discover new places in our city."

— SAM, 54

DIVERGENCE IN LEARNING

Autistic girls can have uneven learning journeys, with extreme highs and lows from subject to subject. This can be attributed to cognitive issues like processing, learning, and memory. Their output can also vary greatly across different subjects owing to differing interests, abilities, and processing styles. Those who are lucky enough to come across a teacher with an awareness of Autism and a desire to make a difference in their lives will undoubtedly find it easier. Sometimes, however, learning success depends on the level of motivation a girl feels and how much she enjoys different subjects.

"I loved history and was obsessed with Philip, Alexander the Great, and Macedonian history. I wanted to do my final year history project on it, but my teachers recommended that I did something more recent because they said that sources would be easier to find. I also loved science, especially Chemistry. This is because my teacher was amazing and he made such an impact on me. When I graduated, I wrote him a thank you letter because I think there is no way I would have done so well if he hadn't believed in me."

— MICHELLE, 51

OBTAINING SUPPORT FOR YOUR DAUGHTER

If your daughter is starting school or going to a new school, you can make the transition easier for them by preparing her early. Talk to the staff at school to find out what efforts they take to make kids with ASD more comfortable. For instance, ask if you can bring your child to school beforehand so they can have a tour of the school. It can also help to assign them a buddy for the first days or weeks. In the days leading up to her first day at school, share her future schedule and create social stories so they know what to expect.

If you have the choice between various schools, find out if any have staff who are trained in teaching students with ASD, especially how it manifests itself in girls. Once your child has started, aim to build rapport with her teachers, and let them know about your child's interests, strengths, and challenges, as well as the techniques that work to help her relax.

An experienced and caring teacher can help your child in countless ways—for instance, by pre-teaching the content of lessons or sending you materials you can go through with your child before they are taught at school. Autistic kids often benefit when a teacher:

- Uses visuals in class.
- Understands that if a child does not respond the way neurotypical kids do, it's not because they want to cause trouble. Most kids want to learn and be liked by their teachers.
- Understands that Autistic kids can have language processing difficulties.
- Gives your child specific, clear instructions, both when speaking to her and handing her written material.
- Gives your child exact guidelines on aspects such as the content, length, priority, and time frames they need to be aiming for.

- Is happy to adapt assignments, essays, and projects so your child can incorporate their special interests into them.
- Allows your child to take on roles that they are comfortable with when working in a group. For instance, if your child loves graphic design, then in a group project, they can take on that task.
- Doesn't give her so much work that she becomes overwhelmed.

INDIVIDUALIZED EDUCATION PROGRAMS AND 504 EDUCATION PLANS

Individualized Education Programs and 504 Plans have both been developed to support K-12 students with learning challenges, though they work differently and are governed by different laws. An IEP is narrower in scope in that a child must have one or more of the thirteen disabilities listed in The Individuals with Disabilities Education Act (IDEA) and this disability must affect their ability to learn/their educational performance. Autism is one of the thirteen disabilities mentioned in the IDEA. In order to qualify for it, a child must also need specialized instruction. A 504 plan, meanwhile, applies to children who have any type of disability that interferes with their ability to learn. An IEP plan is formulated by a team that includes the child's parent or caregiver, at least one of their general education teachers, one special education teacher, a school psychologist or other specialist, and a district representative. A 504 plan is determined by people who are familiar with the child, including the child's parent or caregiver, general and specialized education teachers, and the school principal.

IEP plans have set learning goals, including annual education goals, the timing of services, any accommodations and modifications required, how the child will take part in standardized tests, and how they will be included in classes and activities. 504 plans are very different in that they are not standardized. They can include any specific accommodations, sources of support, and services set up to help the child (Understood n.d.).

Team cooperation is key to choosing an appropriate plan. Opting for an IEP essentially means your child will have specialized instructional goals and objectives, while 504 plans do not require specialized instruction. Both aim to support students in their journey toward independence.

GETTING READY FOR SCHOOL ACTIVITIES

Prior to starting school, you may want to try out the following activities with your child (Raising Children n.d.):

- Walking or driving past their new school.
- Visiting the school out of hours.
- Practice eating meals out of a lunchbox.
- Practice putting on and wearing their school uniform (if they will be wearing a uniform).
- Practice useful questions and answers.
- Print out a free social story. The website, AutismLittle-Learners.com has free social stories for children of various ages. They feature images of kids meeting teachers and students, having recess, and having spring breaks and summer vacations. The ABAResources.com site compiles a host of social stories from various sources. They cover a wide array of topics ranging from getting ready for school in the morning to how to use the bus, do schoolwork, walk in the hall, listen to the teacher, take turns, complete work in class, and more.
- Start creating a Transition Plan alongside school staff. This plan can include:

  1. A profile of your child, including their interests, strengths, and updated medical, therapy, and health reports and needs.

2. Activities that can help your child get to know her new school.
3. Appointments for your child to meet staff prior to starting.
4. Visits to school a few days prior to starting, so your child can play a little in the playground, see her classroom, and similar.
5. A photo album with pictures of the school and staff your child will be dealing with.

In this chapter, we have covered the ins and outs of learning and education for Autistic girls. In the following chapter, we will deal with a skill that is vital at school, at home, and in social circles: communication.

U: UNITED AND COMMUNICATIVE

HOW TO UNDERSTAND YOUR CHILD'S MEANS OF COMMUNICATION

> *"Autists are the ultimate square pegs, and the problem with pounding a square peg into a round hole is not that the hammering is hard work. It's that you're destroying the peg."*

— PAUL COLLINS (SCHUMER 2024)

Being Autistic and teaching both neurotypical and neurodivergent kids have reinforced my belief in the importance of being in tune with the many ways in which Autistic children are trying to communicate with parents, teachers, and friends. My friend Lena, a mom at my daughter's daycare, has a three-year-old Autistic son who can pronounce words and name objects but does not ask for what he needs and can't associate the word "mom" with Lena. At the local Autism support group, some parents tell me that their child began communicating with them in a way they understood at the age of five or beyond. Prior to that, flashcards and apps were a huge help. For many children, being understood when they ask their child to take something to their room or fold something away arises after a couple of years of various types of therapy, including occupational therapy.

Many report that when their child starts talking, they don't stop! It is important to celebrate each step of a child's progress and to focus on the daily connections we make with them instead of lamenting that we may have to wait a while before we can have a long conversation involving answers to questions like "How was school today?" "What did you learn?" or "Did anything funny happen today?" To fill these gaps, it helps to build a great relationship with your daughter's teachers and to ask them to fill you in on any amazing moments you might otherwise miss out on.

HOW AUTISM AFFECTS COMMUNICATION

Autistic kids may have difficulty developing language skills and understanding what others are saying. They may also find it challenging to communicate nonverbally, through the eyes, hand gestures, and facial expressions (National Institute on Deafness and Other Communication Disorders, n.d.) and, as mentioned previously in this book, they may find eye contact unnecessary. You may find that an Autistic child:

- Finds it harder to take part in everyday conversations
- Prefers to speak exclusively about their interests and finds it hard to take turns or share
- Is perceived as blunt by others
- Finds the meaning and rhythm of words hard to work out
- Finds it difficult to work out when irony, sarcasm, or humor are being used
- Finds it harder to understand non-verbal language and the subtleties of vocal tones
- Uses rigid or repetitive language
- Speaks eloquently about one topic but then finds it difficult to sustain a two-way conversation
- Has uneven language development (for instance, they may develop a wide vocabulary in one area of interest)

- May be unable to use gestures such as pointing to express meaning

The above list won't necessarily cover your own child's experience, as communication styles and abilities vary greatly from child to child. Some girls can enjoy frequent chatting, while others may be completely silent. As a whole, many parents find that trying to communicate with their child is far more helpful than correcting every single grammar and syntax error. When you concentrate on exchanging ideas, thoughts, wants, and needs, your interactions can be significantly more meaningful.

"I am a gamer and am into Mass Effect, which is a military sci-fi game set in the future. In the game, there is a species called the Elcor, whose speech is heard by others as a flat monotone. When they are talking among themselves, they use subtle body movements, scent, and other specific means of conveying subtleties of meaning, but when they speak with non-Elcor, they prefix all their speech with a statement that clarifies their tone. For instance, they might say 'genuine enthusiasm,' followed by a sentence that seems to lack all traces of enthusiasm. So before every sentence, they might say words like 'Happy and amused,' or 'Impressed.' My oldest daughter Ariana (who is now 17) is Autistic, and she used to misinterpret my tone almost daily. This would lead to many upsets and lots of frustration on her part. We used to play Mass Effect together and one day, I decided to speak Elcor with her, explaining my intention before saying something. She laughed and was delighted by the idea. Speaking like the Elcor doesn't always work, but it has quite dramatically reduced the number of misunderstandings we have."

— BILLIE, 41

STRATEGIES FOR CREATING A LANGUAGE-RICH ENVIRONMENT FOR YOUR CHILD

Observation and experimentation are vital when it comes to helping your daughter communicate. Break down your goals into small steps instead of expecting big changes too soon. For instance, if your daughter cries in her room when she wants you to give her a toy that is up on a shelf, it might be too hard for her to say "toy" or "car." The first step could therefore be pointing at the toy she wants, and then helping her point at it herself. If she already communicates by taking your hand and placing it on what she wants, then you might use words or flashcards when your child pulls your hand toward what they want. For instance, you might say "car" or pull out a flash card with a car. Praise is also useful. Whenever your child demonstrates the communication you are working on, give them praise for it.

Creating a language-rich environment for your child is another key step in honing their communication skills. You can do this in numerous ways, including:

- Verbalizing your thoughts often
- Acknowledging your child's attempts to communicate with you even if you can't work out what they are trying to say to you
- Making a little time every day for reading together
- Telling them stories and making up stories together
- Singing alone and together
- Giving your child time to respond
- Acknowledging that communication is possible, even when they (or you) don't say a word
- Using short, clear sentences
- Asking your child questions
- Talking with them about the topics they are interested in

AUTISM AND PRAGMATIC SPEECH

Pragmatic speech involves communicating appropriately in social settings (or knowing what, how, and when to say something). Autistic people can have pragmatic speech delays. It involves three main skills (Cincinnati Children's, n.d.):

1. Using language for different purposes, for instance:

- Greeting someone: "Hi." "Bye." "See you later." "How was your day?"
- Informing someone of something: "Okay, I'm leaving." "I have class now." "My mom is waiting for me."
- Giving orders or instructions: "Take this to the table." "Pick this up, please." "Say hello."
- Stating something: "I'm going to the library."
- Asking: "Would you like to come with me?" "Do you like strawberries?" "What's your favorite color?"

2. Changing language according to the situation, for instance:

- Talking to a little sister vs. talking to a teacher.
- Speaking in a classroom vs. speaking at a party.
- Talking about a family member to other family members vs. strangers.

3. Following rules for conversations, for instance:

- How to start a conversation.
- How to introduce a new subject.
- Maintaining a conversation that someone has started.
- Understanding and using non-verbal signals to connect with others.
- Taking turns to talk without interrupting others.
- Respecting others' personal space.

When a child lacks pragmatic language skills, they may:

- Not understand the importance of turn-taking in conversations.
- Be unable to read non-verbal cues that others are sending them.
- Not realize that others do not have enough knowledge about a topic they bring up.
- Say unrelated things while someone else is speaking, or be unable to follow the flow of the conversation.
- Not give others the background information they need to make sense of what one is saying. For instance, a child might say something like "She showed me this the other day," without explaining who or what they are speaking about.
- Find abstract language such as jokes or figures of speech difficult to work out.
- Not be able to understand the main topic being discussed or the main gist of a story they are reading.
- Fail to understand where a story or conversation is heading.

Below, I will discuss the usefulness of working with a speech therapist to hone your child's use of pragmatic language. You can also help your child at home in the following ways:

- Practice starting and ending conversations.
- Help your child identify the topic of conversations and stories.
- Use pronouns without letting your child know who the pronoun refers to. This will encourage your child to ask for missing information. It will also help you show how identifying someone is important before using a pronoun to refer to them.
- Practice non-verbal cues like smiling, frowning, rolling the eyes, crossing one's arms, furrowing one's brow, and talking about what each cue means.

- Role playing situations where the child has to talk about the same things to different people (for instance, a sibling, a friend, a teacher, their grandfather, and similar).

WORKING WITH A SPEECH THERAPIST

A speech therapist is trained to treat people with language, speech, and voice issues and they can make a big difference in your child's ability to communicate (Rudy 2024). Typically, speech therapy can begin early (during a child's preschool years) and follows a structured, specialized program that aligns with your child's age and needs. A speech therapist can help your child (Arizona Autism United 2021):

- Express what they want and need, understand what others are saying to them.
- Communicate in a way that others understand.
- Articulate words and sentences clearly.
- Communicate with others so they can develop friendships.
- Hone their speech pragmatics, to help your child understand when specific words or phrases are appropriate to use.
- Help your child work out when it is okay to join a conversation vs. when it is private by observing others' body language.
- Learn how to ask and answer questions.
- Understand prosody (the sound of the voice as it goes up and down in conversations. Autistic kids can sometimes speak in a flat tone. Speech therapy can help them add more "melody" to their words, so their speech is more impactful or easier to connect with).
- Hone their grammar (some Autistic children find it challenging to follow grammatical rules. For instance, they may refer to themselves in the third person).
- How to excel at conversation—vital skills to start, maintain, and end a conversation.

- Sharpen their knowledge of abstract concepts such as "fairness," "justice," "freedom," and similar.
- Social skills such as the appropriate distance to stand from others, how to read the room, and similar.
- Overcome feeding challenges (some speech therapists are trained to address issues such as swallowing in Autistic people).

Speech therapists use numerous techniques, depending on what will work best for a child. They may use visual cues and gestures, a picture exchange communication system, speech output devices, and even massage and exercises to help a child strengthen their jaw, mouth, throat, and lips.

Your speech therapist is another vital member of your team. They will work closely alongside you, often giving you exercises to practice with your child at home. They may also suggest ways that you can communicate more optimally with your child (for instance, by articulating words very clearly) so your child can copy your speech. Getting started on speech therapy early is a good idea, as it will help your child hone numerous skills and help them in their relationships and at school.

SIGN LANGUAGE

Some Autistic kids are non-verbal, as they may find it challenging to connect spoken words to things. They may feel frustrated when others can't understand them, and this can lead to meltdowns and anger. Some find that sign language can help them communicate their wants and needs in a calm but effective way.

Sign language can help children enhance their social skills. Signs can express their thoughts, emotions, wants, and needs clearly, enabling them to feel more empowered and to create meaningful connections with others. The use of signs can additionally play an important role in supporting a child's cognitive development. This is because sign language provides a multisensory experience that can aid in cognitive processing and comprehension (Moller 2024). Research has shown that sign language can also:

- Improve language and vocabulary skills by reinforcing the relationships between signs and their meanings. Signs can help kids understand and retain new words and expand their vocabulary. Using sign language can improve expressive and receptive language abilities. This can help children feel more confident and motivated to interact with others.
- Hone their memory and learning skills. The visual nature of signs can boost memory and support children's understanding and recall of academic content. This is because sign language engages many senses all at once (which aids in cognitive processing) and expands one's vocabulary.
- Help kids manage their emotions. Sign language enables kids to express their feelings more effectively, reducing the frustration and anxiety that arises when they cannot do so verbally. By using signs to describe how they feel, they develop their self-awareness and can take steps to soothe themselves—for instance, when they feel stressed or tired.
- Bridge the communication back. Kids who are non-verbal can feel immensely liberated when they can interact with others through signs.

TYPES OF SIGN LANGUAGE

People on the spectrum may benefit from learning either American Sign Language (ASL) or Signing Exact English (SEE). These languages differ in the respective sentence structures they use. ASL follows a subject-verb-object structure. SEE follows English language rules. It adds prefixes, endings, and verb tenses to offer an exact visual representation of the language. Many professionals recommend the use of SEE for Autistic kids because it replicates English words and therefore does not rely so much on facial expressions to convey meaning

(Delano 2023). However, some people find SEE slower than ASL, and many more people utilize ASL. Because every child has unique needs, it is vital to choose the best fit for them—something your speech therapist can help you out with.

> *"I'm Autistic and Deaf, and I found ASL easy to learn. You don't have to read body language as much because signs have clear meanings. Because the expressions are so obvious, it's kind of easy to work out. Sometimes I think signs can be another type of masking because many of us can just tell when someone is happy, sad, frustrated etc."*
>
> — SVETLANA, 18

> *"The hardest thing about sign language for me is fingerspelling, which is used to spell out names, nouns, places, etc. One way I practice this is to work with my sister and spell words forwards and backwards using fingerspelling. Eventually, you get really fast at it."*
>
> — DIANA, 19

THE THEORY OF DOUBLE EMPATHY

I have met many families with Autistic kids and I occasionally come across parents who are frustrated because children may rely on behaviors such as watching videos, jumping, or twirling repetitively as a means of self-soothing. Some have told me that when their child spends a lot of time watching videos, they feel like they communicate with family members less. Autistic children communicate all the time, and when they watch videos as a means to stim, it is probably because they are obtaining great enjoyment from it or trying to de-stress and regulate themselves.

The world can seem tough at times because first, it labels your child as having a "problem." Next, it expects you to "fix" it so that your child behaves "like everyone else." It should be them, not your child, who learns to adapt, accommodate, and accept. For an Autistic person, daily life can feel like someone has taken them from their world and whizzed them off to another one where a different one is spoken. Everybody expects them to automatically understand this foreign language and gets frustrated when they take time to do so. Imagine how you would feel if you were in this situation. As parents, we can make it easier on our child and ourselves by focusing on our child's wants and needs, instead of trying to somehow "fix" her so the rest of the world "copes" better.

This brings us to the Theory of Double Empathy, which suggests that the traditional depiction of empathy as being a one-way street is mistaken. This theory challenges the dominant narrative that Autistic people need to be "cured" to function in society. It argues that they are no less empathetic than neurotypical people. Instead, the difficulty in understanding and empathizing with others is a two-way street. The aim, then, is to create an environment in which neurotypical and Autistic people can communicate and see things from each other's point of view. This theory highlights the need for neurotypical people to make efforts to accommodate the communication styles and sensory needs of Autistic people. For instance, they can make a big difference by simply using direct language, avoiding irony, and adjusting the sensory environment (Zauderer 2023).

SPEECH THERAPY ACTIVITIES YOU CAN TRY AT HOME

To boost your child's communication skills, try the following activities at home (Stamurai 2021):

- **Animal noises:** Point to images of different animals and encourage your child to imitate the sounds they make. Do the same and turn it into a fun learning and bonding session.

- **Essential words:** Teach your child specific words like "More," "Stop," and "Help," in different situations.
- Reward your child for using new words, responding to their name, or advancing communicating with you more often.
- **Take various colors of the same thing** (such as clothing) and say the colors of the items as you point to them. Encourage your child to choose the items they feel like wearing or playing with.
- **Play sorting games.** You can practice sorting items according to color or size, or play matching games based on these and other attributes. You can use practically any item for this game, including buttons.
- **Seed sorting:** Take various seeds and work alongside your child, sorting them into different groups according to shape, size, and color. You can do the same with beads and any other items you find that are plentiful and colorful. Kids also enjoy playing this game with colored dot stickers.
- **Create a personal communication board.** These boards typically include numerous activities (for instance, reading, going to school, swimming, dancing) and emotions (for instance, a happy face, sad face, angry face). Kids can then match the face with the event to show you which events they enjoy the most.

- **Teach them facial expressions.** There are numerous free online resources showing you different facial expressions. Show each expression to your child and discuss each expression and the emotions it conveys.
- **Play "What's in the bag?"**: Place lots of fun items in a bag and invite your child to ask, "What's in the bag?" to encourage them to ask questions. Keep it up throughout the day, teaching them questions like "Where's Mom?" "Can I play on my tablet?"

Having discussed communication, it's time to turn our attention to special interests. These are a fantastic way to communicate with a child, boost their self-confidence, and create treasured memories together.

SOWING THE SEEDS OF
UNCONDITIONAL LOVE

"Autism doesn't come with an instruction guide. It comes with a family who will never give up."

— KERRY MAGRO

You are now halfway through your reading journey—a fitting time to think about the vast differences between how the world often sees Autism and what it really is. By now, you have seen how so many of the myths surrounding Autism—some of the most prevalent of which are that Autistic kids lack empathy, that they cannot maintain eye contact, or that they have difficulty making friends—have been proven wrong in numerous studies. You have seen how these myths lead to underdiagnoses or misdiagnoses of Autism for many girls, primarily because their symptoms often fall outside the characteristic symptoms attributed to boys.

I would like to reiterate one message from the chapters you have read so far. It is important to stay up to date with the latest research findings. When you know more about the Autistic brain, the differences between behaviors in girls and boys, and the reasons why masking can do such great harm to a child's self-esteem, your confidence as a parent grows exponentially. As an informed parent, you know how much your child can benefit from letting them guide your path in everything from how they communicate with you to the magic of their special interests. If this book helps you clear your doubts, understand your daughter, and embrace strategies that help your child enjoy life to the fullest, then I hope you can share your opinion with other parents.

By leaving a review on Amazon, you'll show other parents of Autistic girls where they can find a comprehensive guide that will help them choose approaches centered on their child's needs.

Simply by sharing what you most liked about the book and a little bit about your own story, you can help others communicate with their child in a profound and meaningful way.

Thanks for your support. Now, it's time for one of the book's most entertaining chapters: fostering your child's special interests!

Scan the QR code to leave your review.

N: NURTURING YOUR CHILD'S PASSIONS

ENCOURAGING YOUR CHILD'S DEEP INTERESTS

> "*Sometimes you hear this phrase, 'To meet the child where the child is.' If this is their natural motivating capacity, then rather than try to suppress it, it might be more helpful to the child to build on it.*"

— ADAM JONES (LABER-WARREN 2021)

My friends with Autistic daughters and sons often say that one of the most fascinating things about their parenting journey is watching how deeply engaged their children are with their special interests. I always tell them that these interests aren't just a childhood thing; they can accompany an Autistic person throughout their lives, providing us with endless enjoyment. Sport has always been one of my deepest interests, but I have developed many interests over the years, some of which last me for just a short period of time. My wife calls me a "Candle-Making CEO" because of my brief but intense fascination with candle-making. It all started when I saw a riveting TikTok video about making candles. I thought, "How hard can it be? If that creator can do it, so can I!" I drove to a supply store some forty-five minutes from home, instead of going to the local arts and crafts shop, and spent $500 on all the supplies that I could possibly think of. I made three batches of candles, and then the dopamine wore off... and I lost all interest in candle-making. I have not touched my supplies in three years, nor do I intend to. My wife regularly brings it up when I start to fixate on something else.

A recent activity I am obsessed with is decluttering: When I get stressed out, I like to throw stuff out that I think I no longer need at that moment—for instance, a sweater in the summer. The fact that winter will be coming again doesn't cross my mind. I just need the sweater gone—out of my life! Since this is not the most effective coping strategy and it has left me cold on more than one occasion, I am working on a different one. Now I have a new fixation—hedging! My gardening knowledge is non-existent, so how was I supposed to know that the big shrubs in front of our house were not hedges but trees and would die if too many of their leaves were removed?

AUTISM AND SPECIAL INTERESTS

Having intense interests can be a source of deep fulfillment and a means to calm down for Autistic girls. You may notice that your daughter has a strong attachment to certain things, or that she enjoys collecting things. She may switch between different interests or remain true to one, and perhaps even study this topic and work in a related occupation when she is older.

The Autistic Self Advocacy Network describes special interests as being "narrow but deep." These interests are highly prevalent among Autistic people; between 75 and 95 percent of us have special interests (Laber-Warren 2021). One 2014 study showed that Autistic people spend around twenty-six hours a week pursuing their special interests. For some kids, special interests can involve repetitive behaviors, such as lining up or organizing their toys. For others, special interests can center around one of the senses, such as hearing. One professor of acoustics from the UK, who is Autistic, recalls that from the time he was a child, he was fascinated by rhythm, words, and parts of tunes.

When he discovered there were degrees in acoustics, he knew exactly what he wanted to dedicate his life to. A 2022 study (Nowell et al. 2020) showed that Autistic kids typically have around nine special interests such as television, things, and music. The mean age of onset of these interests is 5.24 years, with the duration of past interests often exceeding two years.

THE BENEFITS OF ENCOURAGING YOUR CHILD'S SPECIAL INTERESTS

In the past, special interests were shunned by some teachers and therapists, because they believed they could distract kids from their schoolwork. However, recent research has shown that special interest can have a host of benefits, including:

- **Improved Self-Confidence**

Excelling in knowledge or skills in one chosen area can help your child feel more knowledgeable. If she is struggling in other areas of school, her special interests can be no less than a lifeline.

- **Enhanced Communication**

To see the extent to which special interests can enhance your child's life, check out the true story of Pulitzer Prize winner, Ron Suskind, whose son, Owen is Autistic. When he was three years old, Owen went from being chatty to not speaking a word, sobbing frequently, and refusing to eat or sleep. His only solace was Disney animated movies, which he had always enjoyed.

Owen also lost his ability to understand the movies, so he memorized them based on sound alone. His family, determined to communicate with him, began using dialogues from Owen's favorite movies. What they discovered is captured in Suskind's beautiful book, *Life Animated* (Suskind 2014). As the family "transformed" into animated characters, they gained insight into the profound meanings of the myths that have accompanied human beings throughout history, helping them make sense of their lives. They realized that their son had invented a language to express his emotions, teaching his family vital lessons that created an unbreakable bond between them.

Children can also be much more communicative when discussing their personal interests, with studies showing they fidget less, make more eye contact, and utilize a richer vocabulary than when discussing other topics (Winter-Messiers et al. 2007).

- **Emotional Regulation**

Special interests provide kids with a means to manage their emotions and express themselves. A key emotional regulation skill is knowing how to calm yourself down when stress arises. For many children, taking part in their special interests enables them to enjoy a mindful pursuit and enjoy a break from the sources of their stress.

- **The Development of Skills**

Taking part in special interests gives children excellent opportunities to sharpen other skills. Say your child is interested in playing music, programming, or building models of houses or cars. These activities boost cognitive, motor, and social skills development. One 2020 study review showed that early music training can help kids improve their inhibitory control (the ability to control their attention, behaviors, thoughts, and emotions). To a lesser extent, it can also hone their working memory and cognitive flexibility.

• **Sheer Enjoyment**

Although research backs this point, you ultimately need to simply speak to Autistic people around you and ask them what their special interests mean to them. For most, their special interests are profoundly entertaining, rewarding, and self-affirming. I asked a few friends to tell me what their special interests mean to them, and am sharing their answers below:

> *"I'm a therapist and I work with many Autistic kids. Through them, I have discovered so many amazing topics like the amazing life stories of athletes, old movies, baking, and so many more things. I can see how much kids enjoy talking about the things they are passionate about, and being curious around them makes for fascinating discussions."*
>
> — NICHOLAS, 53

> *"I am a big Miley Cyrus fan and have been following her since I was 11. I was into Hannah Montana. I used to ask my dad to record all the episodes, so I could watch them. I used to learn the lines from the show and see what Miley was wearing and try to dress similarly. Now that I am older, I realize that the show was so meaningful to me because I could relate to the main character, who played a pop star pretending to be a typical high school kid. She also had to wear a mask and act like she was someone else. The show also helped me learn words and mimic the way the characters would talk to each other."*
>
> — INGRID, 31

> *"I love animals and nature, especially horses. It is hard for me to describe why I love them so much. I guess it is because they are so majestic and beautiful. They are so large and powerful*

yet gentle and they seem to know how you are feeling. I started riding at the age of six. Since I rode my first horse, I developed an interest in them and began studying all the different breeds and drawing them. I want to study to become a veterinarian when I am older. I would love to work with horses. I already feel connected to them, but I want to know everything there is about their behavior and psychology, and I want to help horses who may have been abandoned or neglected."

— ZARA, 16

AUTISTIC GIRLS AND SPECIAL INTERESTS

Every child can develop special interests in unexpected topics, but research does show that the following areas of interest are more prevalent among Autistic girls and women (Autism Awareness Australia, n.d.):

- Animals
- Music, arts and crafts, and literature
- Fiction and science fiction
- Fantasy
- Nature
- Animanga and gaming
- Psychology
- Social justice (including disability and women's rights)
- Celebrities

Of course, many girls enjoy games traditionally deemed "boys' games."

 "I love Pokémon, Legos, and remote control vehicles. Why do they have to call them toys for girls or boys?"

— SAMANTHA, 15

"I love Marvel Comics and characters and enjoy dressing up as my favorite characters."

— ELIZABETH, 9

HOW TO ENCOURAGE YOUR DAUGHTER'S SPECIAL INTERESTS

Kids can have numerous activities competing for their time these days, during and after school. As parents, it is typical to want a child to take part in various activities. However, giving Autistic girls the time they need to pursue their interests meaningfully is vital.

Encouraging your child's special interests begins by adopting a curious, open mindset and not judging why, how, or when they indulge their interests. It continues with you showing an interest in the things they love. You can do this by:

- Asking them questions about their interests, doing a little research of your own into them, and sharing the information and resources you find.
- Listening actively as they talk about their hobbies, without cutting them off or changing the subject.
- Creating plans around their interests. For instance, if they love dogs, they may enjoy visiting a shelter and walking or grooming the dogs on weekends. If they are into nature, then a camping trip or a picnic in a green area may be exactly what they need for a happiness boost.
- Accessing audiovisual material about their special interest and watching or listening to relevant media together.
- Buying them toys, books, and any materials they might enjoy that are related to their interest.
- Creating a project together.
- Seeing unfinished projects as a good use of time, not a waste. Your child is picking up so many skills as they take part in

activities related to their interest. Above all, these interests help them battle stress and lose themselves in a world that is deeply fulfilling and interesting for them.

SPECIAL INTEREST ACTIVITIES

Choose a weekend idea that taps into your child's special interest. The following are ideas they may enjoy. Your daughter can also be a direct source of ideas for fulfilling activities.

- Volunteer with a group that specializes in your child's area of interest. Ideas include beach or park clean-ups, volunteering at an animal center, taking part in food programs, or being part of an aged and disability visitor program. In the US, sites like Volunteer.gov will provide you with a host of fun volunteering ideas.
- Create a project together. It could be a collage, scrapbook, sculpture, musical tune, cartoon, animation, graphic design or other project that centers on your child's interests. A good idea is to learn skills like photo editing and graphic design using free online tools for beginners.
- Draw fantasy characters, design and sew a costume, and visit a local anime or book convention.
- Go hiking or walking if your child derives satisfaction from the natural world.
- Make a pop-up book that focuses on your daughter's interests. There are many online sites (including wikiHow) that can take you through all the steps of creating a pop-up book.

Special interests are always more fulfilling when they are shared. Having a curious mindset will take you far when it comes to connecting with your child based on shared interests. Whenever your child demonstrates an interest in an activity, try to think of how you can take it beyond books. Think about ways to make their interest more vibrant for them. For instance, if they love art, they may love taking part in a workshop that teaches them how to use a specific medium or specific materials. If they are into horses, then they will undoubtedly enjoy having horse riding lessons. Without a doubt, the emotional satisfaction that their interests will bring them will help your goal in the next chapter: that of helping them regulate their emotions.

❶: INVESTING IN EMOTIONAL WELL-BEING

STRATEGIES FOR MANAGING EMOTIONS

"If I could snap my fingers and be non-autistic, I would not. Autism is part of what I am."

— DR. TEMPLE GRANDIN (TOBIK 2021)

Emotional regulation is the ability to use healthy strategies to deal with negative emotions like stress and anxiety. Anyone can have difficulty with this skill; in fact, around 32 percent of people surveyed say they have a close friend or family member who has anger management issues (Counselling for Kids, n.d.). However, Autistic people are more likely to struggle with managing their emotional states. One study showed, for instance, that Autistic kids and teens are four times more likely to have challenges managing their emotions than their neurotypical counterparts (Conner et al. 2021).

One of the stereotypes of Autism is that we are unfeeling and cold, and that reason rather than emotion rules us. Sometimes I wish this misconception was partially true because I feel emotions in immense waves and I sometimes don't know how to deal with them. I have a profound sense of empathy for people who are suffering and when I feel that they have been wronged, I get furious. When I was a child, my emotional regulation was practically non-existent and I raged very quickly. I had a strong sense of justice and simply couldn't accept things I deemed unjust. My youth was, in large measure, marked by the sense that I was powerless against the tsunami of emotions that came over me; the idea of being able to control or manage them seemed impossible. I would dwell on tough incidents for days; they would consume me and ruin my days and weekends sometimes. I would spend far more time raging about the way someone had treated me than was healthy and it took me a long time to feel like I wasn't being consumed by my emotions.

Time has improved my ability to manage my emotions, and today, I know myself better. I know my triggers, and I know that time and finding things that soothe me can take me far. A good friend once told me that it made little sense to worry so much about something someone had done when those who have wronged you may not even be spending two minutes worrying about it. By allowing myself to be consumed by emotions, I was essentially giving them power over my life, and that is something I no longer have the time or energy to do. In a way, being a mom has taught me to prioritize not only my time but also my mental energy. I need to be my best self for my family and that means knowing what's worth worrying about. Despite what I have learned over the years, I feel for girls and teens who find emotional regulation hard to master.

WHY EMOTIONS ARE SO CHALLENGING FOR AUTISTIC GIRLS

It is thought that Autistic people find emotional regulation challenging because of differences in arousal systems in the brain. Add to this the sensory and social challenges we face, and it can result in more frustration and stress (Sarris 2022). Another issue that can impact emotional regulation in Autistic people is alexithymia—an impaired ability to be aware of, identify, and describe one's emotions. As a result of all these factors, meltdowns and a feeling of being overwhelmed can be more frequent.

DIFFERENCES BETWEEN GIRLS AND BOYS

A 2020 study (Wieckowski et al.) on gender differences among young Autistic people hospitalized for psychiatric issues found that girls can find emotional control harder than boys, and that these differences are small but significant. Emotional dysregulation is something that should be taken seriously, because it is linked to problems with social skills later in life and a higher risk of depression and anxiety.

In the study, girls scored higher for emotional reactivity than boys at all ages (from four to twenty years of age). They also scored higher in terms of depressed mood, with the gender gap growing above the age of thirteen. A similar gap exists among neurotypical people as well, so the researchers stated that it was unclear whether Autism predicts issues with emotional regulation any more than sex or gender. They postulate that there is a gender baseline difference, and the distance from the baseline is the same for Autistic males and females. One reason suggested for why girls fare worse is that they are diagnosed later. Other factors such as abuse and family composition could also worsen the problem, though further study on the effect of these factors is necessary.

ALEXITHYMIA AND ITS EFFECTS ON EMOTIONAL REGULATION

Alexithymia is a word used to describe the difficulties that people can have with describing the emotions they are feeling. Around 4.89 percent of neurotypical people have alexithymia, compared to 49.93 percent of Autistic people (Emily, n.d.). Alexithymia is linked to interoception (the ability to identify, comprehend, and respond to internal body states). As previously discussed, interoception allows us to identify when we are feeling hungry, thirsty, cold, hot, and similar. When we are unable to identify these needs, life can become a lot tougher.

People who have alexithymia experience it in different ways. For instance, some may find excitement or sadness easy to identify but struggle to figure out anger or frustration. Some may sense that something is not right, but be unable to say exactly why.

Identifying emotions is one of the key steps of emotional regulation because when you know what you're feeling, you can take steps to fulfill the need it is producing. For instance, if you know you're hungry, then you can prepare a meal. If you know you are cold, you can grab a blanket and warm up. If you are furious about something, you know that taking a little break can help. If you are in the middle of a discussion with someone and things are getting heated, you can agree to cool down and discuss it a bit later in the day or at another time. When you don't know that you're feeling angry, however, you can stay in that situation longer than is healthy and things can simmer and boil until the lid of the pressure cooker goes flying off. In time, you can lose faith in your own ability to deal with tense situations, and frequent outbursts can impair your relationships.

Alexithymia can also make it harder to express and interpret other people's emotions. We may be feeling an emotion without expressing it the way a neurotypical person might. This is why we so often feel the need to "mask." We realize that in order for others to understand we are feeling a certain way, we have to "wear" the right expression. We may be feeling anger, for instance, yet others may look at us and think we are perfectly okay.

The same goes for others' emotions. Because much of how we interpret others' emotions comes from studying certain gestures, we may think someone is mad when they are furrowing their brow, even if they are simply concentrating on something. Not all is gloom and doom, however. You can turn alexithymia into a strength by using it as a reason to ask people how they feel instead of just assuming their emotional state. It may come as a surprise, but there are many maskers out there… it's not just Autistic people who seem okay when they may be upset inside. As your daughter matures, share information about alexithymia with her and let her know that she can overcome this obstacle by simply checking in with others more often.

If alexithymia is or continues to be a problem for your child, therapy can also help and it is worth considering. This is because failing to express what we feel or identify what our loved ones feel can cause chasms in a relationship. For instance, if your partner is deeply frustrated or upset and you cannot perceive this, over time, they may feel unloved even though this is as far from the truth as it could be. They may also feel like a sense of connection is missing if you don't share your emotions with them; it could feel like you are repressing or hiding important information they would like to know. Therapy can help you hone your emotional awareness, because it is just a skill, like many other factors that make you emotionally intelligent.

HOW TO HELP YOUR DAUGHTER COMPLETE A TASK SHE IS HAVING DIFFICULTY WITH

It can be useful to teach your child a few phrases they can use when they are finding a task challenging. Take a starting phrase like "It would be good if…" then show her a few endings to the phrase such as:

- "you could help me."
- "a friend could help me."
- "I could work alone."
- "I could work with _____."
- "I could work somewhere quiet."
- "I could do this another way."

Let your daughter know that she can use the means of communication she most prefers to share what she wants with you. For instance, she may prefer to sign, draw, or search for something online and show it to you.

YOUR DAUGHTER IS NOT TRYING TO ANNOY YOU

"I can't" is different from "I don't want to," yet sometimes, people can confuse the two when it comes to Autistic kids. Imagine that you ask your daughter to pick up her toys because it's bath time. She might keep playing with the toys even though you repeat the request for her to finish. When she does this, it can feel like she is resisting you, being difficult, or deliberately trying to irk you. We have spoken of so many differences in the way the Autistic brain works. For instance, perhaps when you told her to put her things away, she filtered out some words and retained just a few. Perhaps she didn't fully understand what you wanted, or she finds it difficult to understand a routine you are trying to establish. Her motor skills might not be up to scratch and she may find it hard to fit her toys into different compartments or tie something up in a bundle before putting it away.

Sometimes, as parents, we can expect all our kids to work at the same pace, but your child may need more time, or simply find what you are asking too complicated. Perhaps her siblings are in her room, they are making noise, and she is trying to avoid sensory overload. Or she might just be hungry or fatigued and not be able to identify or express how she feels. It pays to give your child the benefit of the doubt in these moments; to assume that she cannot do something instead of assuming that she doesn't want to do what you ask.

AUTISTIC GIRLS ARE EMPATHETIC

Of the many myths that accompany Autistic people, one of the most harmful is the one saying we aren't empathetic. I mentioned that difficulties with expressing what we feel and understanding what others do can be mistaken for a lack of interest. When I hear someone say Autistic people are unfeeling, I often think, "Oh, I wish I felt things less intensely." The truth is that many Autistic people report feelings of excessive empathy. One 2022 study (Shalev et al.) found that Autistic people have lower total empathy but higher empathic disequilibrium (higher emotional than cognitive empathy).

Emotional empathy allows us to feel another person's emotions deeply. For instance, if we see someone crying, we may feel their sadness profoundly. Where we may not do so well is in cognitive empathy—having "complete and accurate knowledge about the contents of someone's mind, including how they feel." In other words, we may find it harder to know what someone's emotional state is at a given time (Lesley University, n.d.). One previous study suggested an interesting hypothesis: our high emotional empathy may cause over-arousal… in other words, we may become overwhelmed by others' emotions. Perhaps our lower cognitive empathy is an adaptive response that helps protect us from this overarousal (Smith 2017).

The 2022 study also showed some sex differences. The researchers found that Autistic females displayed emotional empathy dominance more strongly than Autistic males. They also concluded that empathic imbalance (between cognitive and emotional empathy) is something that does not uniquely affect Autistic people.

Empathy is something that can be learned. As a parent, you can help your child master this quality by modeling empathic behavior and prompting your child to notice emotional states in others. You can reinforce the usefulness of responding to another person's emotions with a phrase, tone of voice, and body language that helps them feel understood and cared for.

HOW TO HELP YOUR DAUGHTER IF SHE IS HAVING A MELTDOWN

School, social pressures, sensory overload, and the pressure to "mask" can all contribute to your child becoming overwhelmed and having a meltdown. Kids and teens who have meltdowns may experience physical sensations like breathing difficulties, blurry vision, and heat in their bodies. A meltdown is not the same thing as a tantrum because it is not a matter of your child wanting to have their way, and it is something that feels totally out of their control. It is just one manifestation of a child's discomfort. Instead of having a meltdown, they may shut down or avoid situations that distress them.

OBSERVING EARLY SIGNS OF A MELTDOWN

To help your child deal with meltdowns, start by being observant and encouraging them to notice the signs that a meltdown is about to take place. They may show signs of anxiety, rocking, walking back and forth, asking repetitive questions, or becoming totally still. At this point, it is important to act fast. A meltdown may be prevented through tactics such as distraction, fidget toys, music, and the elimination of triggers. Parents can help prevent a meltdown by remaining calm.

IDENTIFYING TRIGGERS

As the months and years go by, it will become easier to know your child's triggers; the things that overwhelm, tire, and stress them out. Keeping a diary can be handy. Record what was occurring right before, during, and after signs of distress. Try to see what connects different meltdowns... for instance, they may often happen at a specific time, after an activity, or in the presence of groups. Common triggers include routine changes, anxiety, and communication blocks. Once you identify your child's triggers, you can take steps to reduce them.

PRACTICING COPING STRATEGIES

Once you notice your daughter is getting frustrated or angry, try the following steps:

- Check if you can do something to help, such as go to a quieter place, remove music that is playing, or offer your child noise-canceling headphones until an unavoidable noise has stopped. Other strategies such as lowering the light, using sensory equipment like glasses with dark lenses, a weighted blanket, and other support tools may also be helpful (National Autistic Society, n.d.).
- If you think it will be helpful, guide them to a quiet spot with low-level lighting.
- Suggest specific activities to your child such as going for a walk, having some food, or playing with a toy they like.
- Offer to practice a relaxation technique such as breathing with your child.
- Be wary of offering too many suggestions. Now is a time for a couple of quiet suggestions and plenty of calm.
- Remain calm and simply be with them.

CALMING TOOLS

I have to admit to being fascinated by all the tools available nowadays. I wish I had had some of these when I was growing up! Once you jump into the Internet rabbit hole of sensory toys, I can guarantee you will probably emerge with a big shopping list. Take the time to enjoy finding items you think your child might enjoy. Just a few sensory tools I saw that caught my eye included visual ones like a turtle with a light that creates underwater effects on the ceiling and plays soothing sounds—this tool is ideal for bedtime. There are also noise-canceling earplugs, weighted pressure vests, stuffed toys that provide calming deep pressure, sensory pillows, hammock swings, and massaging neck pillows to select from.

I find that it pays to experiment and try out various tools. Your child may take more strongly to one of them, but hopefully, they will enjoy the different toys, apps, and devices you provide them with at different stages of their childhood. It also pays to have chewy or crunchy snacks on hand. Oral proprioceptive input can help calm your child down, and sometimes, kids can get cranky simply because they are hungry! Bring a few unscented hand wipes with you as well. Your child may feel overwhelmed if they touch something that remains on their hands. Give them a chance to wash their hands or wipe any stains or bothersome substances away. If your child has a preferred hand lotion or cream, bring it along. The same goes for any essential oils they enjoy smelling. Fragrance can be a powerful way to calm the mind, so long as the particular scent is one your child enjoys.

VISUAL SCHEDULE EXERCISE

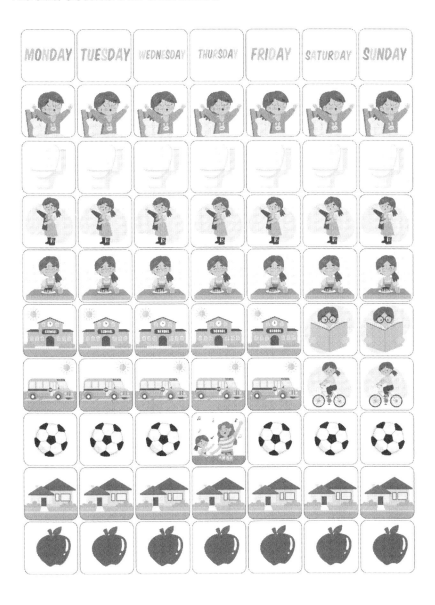

If you know you will be veering from your daughter's usual routine (for instance, if you have to travel, visit someone after school, or start a new therapy or activity), make a visual schedule board or poster various days in advance, so your daughter knows she will be experiencing this change soon. Represent their daily schedule with pictures. Sites like Do2learn.com provide free print cards encompassing various activities. Your vision board might include activities like getting up, going to the bathroom, getting dressed, having breakfast, going to school, being picked up, visiting a new therapist, then coming home, having a snack, and so forth. You can break up the new activity into many smaller steps. For instance, you might provide an image of your child going to the therapist's office, talking to them, and then doing exercises. Apple like Visuals2Go are perfect for this task, as they contain an array of templates and cards that you can print out.

Emotional regulation is an important skill children need to enjoy a sense of inner peace and calm. It is also vital for getting on with others... which brings us to our next chapter, which is all about social interaction.

: TOGETHERNESS AND RELATIONSHIPS

HELPING YOUR AUTISTIC DAUGHTER MAKE AND SUSTAIN MEANINGFUL FRIENDSHIPS

> *"Don't ever, EVER compare yourself to a neurotypical girl or woman. They are a different species and you'll only feel inadequate and bad about yourself. Find your tribe—online, in groups at comic conventions. Find people who are delighted that you are you. And you should be delighted that you are you too because when you're 70, you'll still be skateboarding, you'll look amazing (from all those years of not ruining your skin with make-up) and you'll realize that all those things you worried about don't matter at all."*
>
> — SARAH HENDRICKX (2015)

Emotional regulation is closely tied to our ability to make and sustain friendships but that is just one piece of the puzzle. Understanding other people, the norms of social groups, and how these unwritten rules vary from group to group is so incredibly challenging. Most of the time, it makes me not engage in social situations; I either avoid them or act like the class clown, so I can direct how the conversation flows. This usually leaves me exhausted and when I come home, I need long periods of rest, silence, and darkness to recover. This makes parenting very difficult.

I counter this by rehearsing social interactions, and I have become so good at it that I don't really know when I'm doing it anymore. For example, when I take my eldest daughter to playgroup, I practice the social norm script of "Hi, how are you going, how has your week been," and similar. I find something to compliment them on or say something positive about their kid. Lots of smiling, lots of expression, lots of eye contact (Meet #Ultramask).

I also plan how I'll regulate once playgroup is over. This typically means running errands until my daughter looks sleepy. Then I quickly put her in the car, she falls asleep, and I have time to get drive-through coffee and listen to my favorite music (hint: it isn't The Wiggles!).

THE TOLL TAKEN BY MASKING

To best understand why masking takes a heavy toll, it pays to see all it involves. Masking can include one or more of the following behaviors:

- Faking eye contact or forcing it during conversations
- Imitating smiles and other facial expressions
- Mimicking gestures
- Hiding or minimizing personal interests
- Rehearsing greetings or responses to questions
- Scripting conversations
- Pushing through intense sensory discomfort such as loud noises
- Hiding stimming

Masking can impose a heavy psychological toll on Autistic people. Those who mask frequently or repeatedly throughout their daily lives can have worse mental health outcomes, including a heightened risk of depression and anxiety, suicidal thoughts, and Autistic burnout. As stated by The Century Foundation's Alex Ashley Fox (2023), the costs of masking reach beyond childhood and affect Autistic people's mental health and work performance when they are adults.

Fox points out that Autistic employees work optimally when they have the right accommodations for their needs. When organizations fail to provide these accommodations, they lose out on hundreds of millions of dollars of potential profits. This is because Autistic employees are forced to invest so much cognitive energy in masking. When they are given support, they can invest their energy where it really counts—in areas like creativity, innovation, and sheer productivity. Autistic people benefit from a high degree of self-determination. However, this is something that can be so difficult, particularly at school, where large classes and minimal staff mean that "rules must be followed," often at the expense of Autistic kids. Many feel that they must either mask or risk being bulldozed by a lack of empathy and an inadequate educational system.

SOCIAL CHALLENGES FOR AUTISTIC GIRLS

Autistic girls can find peer relationships difficult to work out. Although they want to experience friendships the way others do, they may not have the innate skills required to do so. They often attempt to mask these challenges by observing and imitating other children. Some can grow very close to just one child, finding it difficult to expand their circle or simply not desiring to. Others can flitter between groups, spending too little time with any one group to become a member of it and create strong bonds with others. Some of the Autistic girls I know have friends but tend to let their friends lead the way instead of starting conversations or friendships themselves.

Many Autistic girls and women feel the same about social interaction as I do. They find them draining because of how much energy it takes to keenly study so many things all at once—people's facial expressions, tone, words, body language, and more… it can get even more frustrating when despite all that effort, you still get nuances wrong or don't get someone's irony or sarcastic humor. Another challenge is when others assume that you are being rude or not following instructions because you are deliberately being difficult. Trying repeatedly without seeing results erodes your self-esteem and self-confidence. It seems like you are constantly questioning yourself. Even when you have friends, you may be unsure if you do.

Research has shown that although Autistic girls have more social motivation than Autistic boys, they have difficulties in recognizing reciprocal friendships during mid-childhood. From about middle school onward, they also report higher levels of frequent loneliness than their neurotypical peers. Right through to adolescence, they additionally tend to have fewer friends.

One theoretical explanation for the reduced level of friendship reciprocity and quality is Milton's double empathy problem, which I mentioned in Chapter Six. Both Autistic and non-Autistic kids can have trouble understanding each other's thoughts, emotions, wants, and needs. Both groups also tend to rate their mutual friendship to be lower in closeness, security-intimacy, and the provision of help.

MORE GENDER DIFFERENCES

In a 2023 study (Libster et al.) published in the journal *Molecular Autism*, researchers focused on how Autistic and non-Autistic boys and girls defined the meaning of friendship. They found that girls were more likely than boys to refer to personality (for instance, mentioning that friends were those who were nice people). Although they referred to qualities like kindness when defining what friendship means, they were not necessarily treated kindly by their friends. Some girls in the study mentioned, for instance, that their friends bullied them and others. The researchers postulated that Autistic kids may find it harder to identify relational aggression within their friendships. For this reason, their parents may need to talk with them about what "true friendship" looks and feels like. Teachers and school staff can also play a key role in identifying bullying behaviors and putting a stop to them.

The study additionally showed that Autistic and non-Autistic boys and girls were equally likely to talk about companionship when defining friendship. They were also equally likely to mention qualities like dependability and intimacy. However, intimacy is a complex construct that doesn't appear until adolescence. The study also showed that as IQ and age increased, so did the likelihood of referring to intimacy when talking about friendship.

Another important finding was that children in middle school tended to be more indiscriminate when selecting friends than older kids. That is, some may deem everyone in the class to be their friend. This changes as kids mature and they begin to develop a more complex idea of what friendship is. This is why making friends can be harder for Autistic kids when they hit adolescence. It can also increase the likelihood of them feeling lonely. In the study, even kids who reported having at least one friend often said they felt lonely. This suggests that the quality and/or quantity of friendships enjoyed by Autistic kids are often not high enough to combat loneliness.

AUTISM AND MISCONCEPTIONS ABOUT ATTACHMENT STYLES

In psychology, the term "attachment" can be defined as the emotional connections infants form with their primary caregivers. British psychiatrist, John Bowlby and American psychologist, Mary Ainsworth, who pioneered attachment theory, espoused that the quality of these early connections determines how you relate to other people and respond to intimacy in your adulthood (Cherry 2023). For instance, if your primary caretaker made you feel loved and safe, then you are most likely to form secure bonds with others. On the other hand, when children are brought up by a caregiver who is abusive, neglectful, or inconsistent, they are more likely to form insecure attachments when they grow up. According to attachment theory, there are four attachment styles:

- **Secure:** Those with a secure attachment style have a good sense of self-worth. They feel comfortable expressing their needs, are emotionally balanced, and are resilient against life's curveballs. They seek closeness from others but do not get overly anxious when they are not with them.
- **Anxious:** Those with an anxious style may want to get close to others but, because their trust has been broken, they find it hard to trust others. They may find it hard to observe boundaries, viewing the space between them and their loved ones as something negative. They need constant reassurance and may be described by others as "clingy."
- **Avoidant-dismissive:** Those who have this attachment style behave in an opposite way to those with an anxious style. They are fiercely independent and tend to distance themselves when someone tries to get close to them. They may minimize others' feelings, keep secrets from them, or have affairs. Likewise, they think that they don't need intimacy to be happy.
- **Disorganized:** People with this attachment style may find close relationships confusing or unsettling. They may be insensitive to others, controlling, or untrusting, and can display negative or antisocial behaviors. Although they crave closeness, they may feel unworthy of love or scared of getting hurt.

Autistic girls are at a higher risk of developing one of the three insecure attachment styles, because they may be misunderstood or rejected by their caregivers. As noted by Devon Price (2022), Autistic kids may be punished or neglected because they do not seek comfort in the "expected" way. Moreover, their attempts at connection (such as playing beside someone without using eye contact) can be mistaken for a lack of interest in connection. Meltdowns, too, can make children seem anxious. After having their attempts at connection rejected or misconstrued various times, Autistic kids can develop insecure attachment styles and others may erroneously deem us to be incapable of creating healthy bonds. Price adds that continual rejection can lead Autistic people to doubt people's attempts at connecting with them. After being misjudged, labeled, and rejected, it can be hard to accept a compliment or see someone's efforts at getting close as genuine.

ENCOURAGING YOUR CHILD TO MAKE HEALTHY FRIENDSHIPS

Insecure attachment styles and bullying or unkind behaviors from peers may lead a child to get close to people who are not true friends and to reject those who have a genuine interest in them. This is especially true if your child has an avoidant attachment style, which can prompt them to become uncomfortable when someone tries to get too close. As a parent, you cannot choose friends for your children, but you can help to get them thinking about what real friends are like.

FRIENDSHIPS WITH OTHER AUTISTIC CHILDREN

Several studies have shown that Autistic people feel more comfortable and more competent when interacting with other Autistic people. Once again, we can turn to the double empathy conundrum, which shows that Autistic and non-Autistic people struggle to understand each other. Autistic people may misinterpret neurotypicals. The latter may do the same and believe the worst of their Autistic peers.

According to a study by Crompton et al. (2020), Autistic people tend to find interactions with other Autistic people less tiring, less stressful, simpler, more familiar in terms of communication styles, and easier to understand. That is, it can be easier to work out what their Autistic friends mean when they communicate. There is also a greater sense of belonging and understanding; of being accepted and not having to mask (Meyer n.d.).

CREATING OPPORTUNITIES FOR SOCIALIZATION

Creating opportunities for your child to connect with other kids—both neurotypical and Autistic—can lead to wonderful connections that are a big source of support and joy for your child. You can help foster new connections by:

- Helping your child understand what friends are (you may find it useful to explain that friends are those who are kind and accepting and who do not judge you or make you feel bad for being yourself).
- Relying on social stories and other visual tools to point out useful things to say or do during social interactions.
- Embracing a growth mentality (even if one playdate goes badly, continuing to organize more playdates) and emphasizing the importance of practicing skills.
- Surrounding your daughter with children with shared interests.
- Seeking therapeutic support, if despite trying numerous strategies, your child is still struggling.
- Joining a support group for parents and families of Autistic children.
- Speaking with your child's school and/or teachers about social goals they can help your child aspire to.
- Planning weekend and extracurricular activities with friends and family.
- Accept your child's wants and needs. They may prefer to just have one close friend or be in a small group. Some may make a sibling their "special interest" and not really want to socialize outside the home.

"I was able to connect with my classmates through gaming. I knew a lot about tricks to win games, so my classmates and I created an online group, and we would play every weekend."

— MANUELA, 15

"One thing I find really hard is when people assume things about me. My intentions are often misinterpreted, and some people think I have bad intentions when I don't."

— MALIA, 38

"I'm not great at small talk. When people start talking about their pets, TV shows, school and other things, I get bored and get lost in my own thoughts. I am not really interested in talking. What really fulfills me is doing things together like going to the beach and kayaking, cycling with someone, or cooking. I want to be with people who watch out for me and help me, and I don't think talking gives you that."

— ADRIENNE, 43

Fascinating Fact: A study by Kuo et al. (2013) found that Autistic adolescents often report spending the most time with their friends playing video games, watching TV, or taking part in structured physical activities. Those who do play video games with their friends are more satisfied with their friendships than those who do not. Another study (Goddard & Cook 2021) found that joining clubs centered on their interests helped them make friends and form meaningful connections. This research highlights why it is so important for parents to encourage their child's special interests.

ENSURE YOUR CHILD'S PHYSICAL AND SEXUAL SAFETY

As your child grows and matures, they will spend more time visiting friends and spending time with others in places outside your home. Ensure that they remain physically and sexually safe by:

- Watching out for signs of physical or other types of assault.
- Helping them identify the people they can trust.
- Teaching them about their body and who has access to their private parts.
- Talking about what is acceptable and not acceptable for others to say or do.
- Teaching them the importance of boundaries. Let them know that boundaries can be physical, sexual, spiritual, financial, intellectual, time-related, and more.
- Explaining the difference between safe and unsafe situations. For instance: it is unsafe to go places where there are no people near you. Places to avoid when they are alone include restrooms that are not used by many people, forests and outdoor areas where nobody is around, and similar. It is also unsafe when an adult asks them to go somewhere with them to help with tasks like finding a lost pet. Adults should rely on other adults for help, not on children (Raising Children n.d.).

HELP YOUR CHILD DEAL WITH BULLYING AND CYBERBULLYING

Earlier, I mentioned that Autistic kids face a higher risk of bullying and cyberbullying than neurotypical kids, especially in mainstream schools (Raising Children n.d.). Bullying can have numerous negative effects on Autistic children. It can affect their self-esteem and mental health, stop them from trying to make friends, and even make them scared to go to school (or reluctant to do schoolwork).

Signs to Watch Out For

The signs of bullying can be physical, behavioral, or emotional. Physical signs include bruises, cuts, and scratches. Children who are bullied may also arrive home hungry, as their lunch may be taken by bullies at school. Behavioral signs include not wanting to go to school or get on the school bus, academic decline, and a refusal to attend parties and other social gatherings. Bullying can manifest itself emotionally, meanwhile, through nightmares, crying, worry, and anger or aggression. A child who is bullied may become less talkative about school or have big mood swings. If you notice these changes, gently ask your child about it, using clear, simple language to formulate your questions. You can also use social stories to ask your child if they have been subjected to bullying.

Nipping Bullying in the Bud

If you suspect that bullying is occurring at school, or if your child has directly told you about it, then immediately set up a meeting with your child's teacher and/or the school administration. Ask for the specific strategy or steps they will take to stop bullying. Many schools have tools that are available to kids, including safe places for lunch (such as clubs or the library), designated members of staff kids can talk to about bullying, Autism and neurodiversity awareness programs, opportunities for Autistic kids to interact with others with shared interests, buddy systems, and more. Specific and swift action needs to be taken because bullying can have long-term effects.

At home, teach your child what to do to help avoid bullying, and share techniques on how to deal with bullies. For instance, your child can use the phrase, "Stop that, I don't like it," then immediately report the bullying episode to their teacher. You can write down a note that explains they are being bullied, and your child can show this note to teachers if bullying occurs (Raising Children n.d.). If, on the other hand, your child is displaying bullying behaviors toward others, talk to their school about how you can support them so the behavior stops. Ask about therapy or support that can help your child understand why bullying is wrong, and help them understand how their words and actions can impact others.

WHAT IS A GOOD FRIEND? EXERCISE

In this chapter, I mentioned that it is a good idea to let your daughter know what good friends are like so that they prioritize healthy friendships and avoid rejecting people who have a genuine interest in building connections with them. For this exercise, let them know what you consider to be a good friend. For instance, share that your best friends:

- Support you when you are down and celebrate your successes and happiness.
- Do not call you names or do or say things to make you feel excluded.
- Are honest with you.
- Openly share their thoughts and feelings with you and listen to you when you want to do the same.
- Do not ghost you when you have arguments.
- Are committed to mending your friendship soon after any arguments have occurred.
- Make you feel accepted and loved just as you are.
- Are dependable.
- Keep your secrets as you do theirs.
- Make you laugh and smile, and being with them is fun and fulfilling.

Ask your child to make their own list, or simply talk about the qualities they value.

This chapter has focused on social interaction and your child's school life. In the next chapter, we will turn our eye toward your home life and all the impactful things you can do to ensure your home is a comfortable, happy, safe sanctuary for your child.

E: EMBRACING COMFORT AT HOME

HOW TO CREATE A COMFORTABLE HOME LIFE FOR YOUR DAUGHTER

"When a family focuses on ability instead of disability, all things are possible."

— AMANDA RAY ROSS (CIRCLE CARE SERVICES, N.D.)

Routines are a lifeline when you are Autistic. For many of us, one small change in our routine can make it very hard to complete everything else on our "to-do" lists.

"I always put sweetener into my coffee mug before placing it under the coffee maker. If I don't do so, I'm likely to put my chia seeds into the mug instead of in my pudding bowl. Missing one little part of the routine throws everything out of whack. Because I work different shifts at work, things aren't always exactly the same, but my core routine can't change too much, or I get flustered or have a meltdown."

— DAWN, 54

"I follow the same routine every day—get up, take a shower, have breakfast, then get dressed to go to work—if not, it's easy to forget something."

— JULIA, 23

THE SIGNIFICANCE OF STRUCTURE AND SCHEDULE IN AN AUTISTIC CHILD'S LIFE

There are numerous reasons why routines are so important for Autistic kids (Zauderer 2023). Set schedules offer a child:

- **Predictability:** It is a lot less overwhelming to go to school, enjoy some playtime, or visit a friend's house if they do so regularly.
- **A greater sense of control:** Autistic kids can easily be overwhelmed by too many things going on at once. In their daily lives, they often lack control over what activities adults propose. Creating a routine covering your child's and your family's activities can ensure they know what to expect.
- **Reduced sensory overload:** Your routine can help to reduce sensory triggers for your child. For instance, you can incorporate sensory breaks into your child's routine, practice deep breathing exercises at specific times of the day, and perform tasks (for instance, their homework) in a quiet area of your home.
- **Strengthening connections between you and your child:** Routine helps foster trust and reduce tension… and these are both crucial for building stronger bonds.
- **Boosting cooperation:** Routines give kids the chance to take charge of their activities, which increases their confidence and makes it easier for the whole family to cooperate to get things done.
- **Increasing a child's sense of ownership:** As kids repeat tasks like organizing their things, doing their homework, or taking

a bath, they can make decisions on how these things get done, which can feel very empowering.

- **Reducing conflict and stress:** The great thing about routines is that everyone knows their roles, goals, and procedures. This reduces the likelihood of conflict.
- **Enhancing security and comfort:** Your routine at home can be one of the greatest sources of comfort for your child, especially if they are called upon to brave routine changes and shifts at school or when they are taking part in extracurricular activities.

TIPS FOR CREATING A ROUTINE

Once you plan out the activities and tasks that belong to your routine, cement it by:

- **Creating a visual tool:** At the end of this chapter, I have provided you with an activity for creating a tool you can use daily until your child can complete their routine without even looking.
- **Use rewards:** Make a list of the small treats and items your daughter loves (such as stickers) and give them to her when she completes every step of her routine.
- **Add tasks to the routine gradually:** Doing so will give your child time to cope with the novelty.
- **Use timers:** Try using timers so you can get everything done on time.
- **Be consistent:** It can be hard to stick to a routine strictly, especially if you like to make plans on the spur of the moment. However, for Autistic kids, consistency can make all the difference in a day.

WHY AUTISTIC KIDS CAN FEEL OVERWHELMED BY CHORES

When your child does not do chores, it isn't because they don't want to. Rather, it is most likely because they don't know exactly what is expected of them. I spoke earlier about how executive functioning (which includes skills like organizing, planning, inhibiting inappropriate responses, and paying attention to what someone is saying) is often a challenge for Autistic people. I mentioned that Autistic children can sometimes focus on a specific detail but not see the whole picture. They may also find it hard to organize information or know the order of the tasks they are expected to carry out. Instructions with long sequences may confuse them.

This is where you step in. You can use visual aids and checklists, or print a schedule that your child can consult as frequently as they need to. When introducing your daughter to a new task, give her enough time so she can understand the instructions. Repeat them as often as she needs you to, and offer her help with each stage of the task. If a task is complicated, break it up into smaller, more manageable chunks and add a new step once your child has mastered the previous ones.

COMMUNICATION AND VISUAL SCHEDULING APPS

Apps have become useful tools for parents and kids when it comes to scheduling and creating a visual routine (Little Puddins n.d.). Just a few you may wish to try out are:

- **LAMP Words for Life**

This app is a communication tool based on neurological and motor learning principles. It is symbol-based, but it also contains text to support literacy learning. The app has three vocabulary levels. The first, called, 1-Hit, has eighty-two core words with a symbol. When the user taps on a specific symbol, the app says it out loud. The second level is called Transition. It introduces a second button into the equation to build on the vocabulary learned on the first level. The third level, called Full Vocabulary, has over four thousand words. It allows users to customize their vocabulary, with features that make it easy to expand one's vocabulary. Although the app is focused on vocabulary, its wide array of images and actions can be used to create your visual schedule.

- **iTouchilearn Life Skills Morning Routine**

This app takes your child through typical morning activities and gives them rewards for completing each set task. It is not specifically created for Autistic children, but its catchy music has made it quite popular among parents and kids alike.

- **Verbal Me**

An app with a host of visuals your child can press to express what they want and need.

- **Visuals2Go**

This app allows users to print cards from a wide array of templates. Users can first communicate by clicking on the card they choose, then use the sentence bar to express their desires through spoken language if they wish.

- **Choiceworks**

An app that is specifically catered to help kids following morning, daytime, and evening/nighttime routines. It was created with the support of child development specialists and hospitals. It aims to promote independence, positive behavior, and emotional regulation at home and beyond. Choiceworks has an image library with 180 preloaded images and audio, but you can also add your own images and record your audio for the ultimate customized experience.

TIPS FOR OPTIMAL NUTRITION

The fuel you feed your daughter can be a big source of support, and knowing what choices to make begins by understanding the most common nutritional challenges for Autistic kids. I mentioned that, to this day, I can't stand the texture of fruits. This is typical for kids on the spectrum. They can have strong likes and dislikes when it comes to food, and some kids may also eat smaller quantities than recommended. This can be owing to sensory sensitivity to textures, tastes, and smells. Another issue is medication; some stimulants used with Autism can reduce appetite, leading kids to eat less.

Autistic kids can have gastrointestinal problems such as tummy pain, constipation, and diarrhea, which could be linked to selective eating. Oral and fine motor impairments can also cause issues with swallowing, chewing, and the use of utensils. Children may find frequent changes in their meals, utensils, and environments difficult to handle. They may struggle with novel foods and find it hard to process the similarities and differences of various food choices (for instance, differences in the colors, tastes, and textures of types of cheeses). What's more, because mealtime is inherently such a social activity, anxiety can manifest itself more strongly than at other times of the day.

Restrictive eating and low food intake can cause some kids to have a low body weight or experience substantial weight loss. However, in some cases, eating a narrow range of foods can lead to weight gain, as children may consume a narrow range of high-calorie foods. It can also mean that kids don't get enough iron and vitamins. Research has found that protein and calcium intake are lower among Autistic kids than in typically developing children. Autistic children also have higher rates of iron deficiency and anemia (Önal et al. 2023).

Many dietary interventions have been studied (including different elimination diets, low-carbohydrate diets, nutritional supplements, probiotics, and more). However, as it currently stands, there isn't enough evidence that these dietary therapies are safe and effective for Autistic kids. However, some parents and healthcare providers have obtained positive results from these approaches.

A dietitian can play a key role in recommending a customized nutritional plan for your child. The Academy of Nutrition and Dietetics recommends that parents include a dietitian as part of the team that deals with their child. This professional can help identify food aversions and explain why your child may have them—including texture, smell, appearance, or temperature.

When you first meet your child's dietitian, they will ask a host of useful questions about aspects such as constipation, sleep, skin conditions, and more. They will assess the adequacy of your child's nutritional intake, since deficiencies could be present, even if your child is growing at an appropriate rate. They may then recommend biomedical testing to identify sensitivities and allergies, as well as potential gastrointestinal parasites and viruses or micronutrient deficiencies (The Spectrum, n.d.). A dietitian can work alongside you to address barriers such as restrictive eating, constipation, and under- or over-eating. Part of their work also involves giving you guidance on how to plan and prepare meals.

There are numerous strategies you can utilize at home to encourage your child to widen their nutritional intake. Scheduling meals is one way to lower anxiety around mealtime. When creating your schedule, include the three main meals and two or three snacks per day. Aim to space meals out, leaving a gap of around 2.5 to 3.5 hours between them. Once you create your routine, use a visual schedule to get your child used to it (Marcus Autism Center, n.d.).

TIME	MONDAY	TUESDAY	WEDNESDAY	THURSDAY	FRIDAY	SATURDAY	SUNDAY
7:30	Breakfast	Breakfast	Breakfast	Breakfast	Breakfast	Breakfast	Breakfast
10:00	Snack	Snack	Snack	Snack	Snack	Snack	Snack
12:30	LUNCH	LUNCH	LUNCH	LUNCH	LUNCH	LUNCH	LUNCH
3:00	Snack	Snack	Snack	Snack	Snack	Snack	Snack
6:00	Dinner	Dinner	Dinner	Dinner	Dinner	Dinner	Dinner

Feed your child foods from all five major food groups, including fruits, vegetables, proteins, grains, and dairy. Don't worry if they don't eat everything you place before them. USDA My Plate (n.d.) educational resource, provided by The United States Department of Agriculture, as a basis for foods to prioritize. You can space out foods from different groups, serving three food groups during main meals and two during snack time. Your child should ideally avoid "grazing," or eating small amounts of snacks throughout the day. This can fill up their tummies and make them less likely to consume healthy foods during major mealtimes. Aim to limit access to salty, sugary, and refined foods and soda-based beverages. Opt for whole, healthy foods and offer fruits when your child is in the mood for something sweet.

HOME DESIGN

Another key aspect of your child's happiness and comfort at home is your home's design and layout. Factors to keep in mind include (DiMare 2023):

• **Acoustics**

An Autistic child may find some sounds painful and distressing. If possible, soundproof your home, especially if you live in a busy area where the sound of cars and people outside can interrupt your child's peace. Many parents find that using a sound machine that emits calming, soothing sounds (known as "pink noise") such as leaves rustling, a heartbeat, or rain can be very soothing for a child.

By contrast, some kids find white noise disturbing since it stimulates the brain. Examples of white noise include the humming noise emitted by some air conditioners, fluorescent lights, and static on the radio or TV. To reduce the amount of noise in your home, use items such as rugs, thick pillows, and heavy furniture placed between shared walls. Heavy shelves, a vertical garden, or a closet can help buffer sound. You can also use corkboards to reduce noise.

• **Color**

To design your home, use soft, neutral colors like gray, beige, and cream hues. Other good choices include blue (which is calming, so long as it is not too dark), green (which is also soothing owing to its imitation of the colors found in nature), pink and violet (which evoke warm feelings), and soft oranges (this color, when chosen in a subdued tone, can be comforting. When used in spaces such as dining rooms and kitchens, it may stimulate the appetite).

- **Natural and de-stressing materials**

If you're into design, then you may have heard of the biophilic design movement, which seeks to blur the distinction between indoor and outdoor living. One of its pillars is the use of natural, non-toxic materials such as reclaimed wood furniture and natural organic cotton rugs and mattresses. For a child's comforter, consider a heavy or weighted blanket. When it comes to furniture shapes, select rounded items rather than those with sharp corners, as curved shapes imitate nature and have a calming effect.

- **Layout**

Consider dividing the spaces where your child spends the most time into three areas: one for play, another for focus, and a third spot for calming. The area for focus could be a small nook or corner separated from other spaces with a movable screen, or a small vertical garden. Your child can use this space for reading or listening to music if they like. Your play area can be a garden, playroom, or even a bathtub. Choose a spot that is easy to clean. Your child's calming area can be a spot on the terrace by a garden, a small library, or any other area where they can enjoy a bit of "me time."

- **Lighting**

As mentioned above, fluorescent lighting and Autism aren't a great mix. Their moods are strongly affected by it. When it is very bright, it can hurt their eyes, and when it flickers and hums, it can be distracting and cause great discomfort. LED lighting can be used, but it should be covered so it is less harsh. Use lamp shades over light bulbs and position lighting smartly. Avoid placing a standing lamp on the side of a TV, for instance, since light in the corner of the eye can be a source of sensory distress.

Go for lighting systems that can be dimmed and those that come in a wide range of colors. Use low brightness and dimmable incandescent or halogen lighting with a lampshade or diffuser. Your child may enjoy night lighting such as stars and constellations that move through their room, colored night lights, or lava lamps. Some lamps (or night light projectors) have a remote control that allows you to choose different themes for your lighting, including stars, the ocean, wildlife, and more. You can also try mood lights (which have an appealing warm glow), Christmas lights, Himalayan pink salt lamps, or even a simple night light.

> *"I have replaced all lights at home that have a lighting frequency. They flicker on and off fast and most of us wouldn't notice it, but my daughter does, and it distresses her."*
>
> — SUSAN, 34

> *"I use soft white or warm white lighting because my child is very sensitive to light."*
>
> — NINA, 50

> *"I am not that sensitive to light, but I do prefer being in low-light conditions."*
>
> — SAOIRSE, 43

DESIGNING YOUR CHILD'S BEDROOM

Your child's room is their very own oasis and a place where they can rid themselves of the stress of the day and unwind. Therefore, this space is one of the most important when it comes to Autism-friendly design. All of the above tips for optimal home design apply, but there are a few additional considerations you may find useful:

- **Create separate spaces:** If their room is large enough to be used for playing, sleeping, and studying, follow the above advice on creating separate zones. You might opt for a double-decker bed, for instance, and use the top bunk for reading, or create a built-in desk that is perfect for homework. One corner of your child's room can contain all their toys and the storage furniture where you keep them. Your child's calming spot can be a cloth teepee with cushions and stuffed toys, a place demarcated by plants, or anywhere that your child can feel protected and safe.
- **Choose quiet flooring:** If your child is very sensitive to sound, then avoid flooring that creaks and wakes them up easily. Natural wood is a nice, soft choice, as is carpeting. If you are laying a new carpet, invite your child to feel various varieties so they select the one that is just right for them.
- **Invest in a good storage system:** Organization and tidiness can help create a calm space for your child, so make sure there are numerous places to store things away. Some beds come with pull-out cabinets beneath and to the side of the bed, which can give you a little more space in which to store books, toys, and technology. Choose minimalist over maximalist design styles and ensure that the room is uncluttered. Avoid having a television or other electronics in your child's room, as screens can be too stimulating and addictive.
- **Choose comfortable materials:** Earlier, I mentioned that many Autistic people enjoy using a weighted blanket. Your choice of sheets is also key. Opt for soft cotton sheets with a high thread count. These are soft and lump-free, and they can handle high temperatures—so they are easy to keep clean without breakage. For bedding and indeed all items in your child's room, pick calming colors but do not be afraid to use small pops of color in decorative items or cushions. Avoid patterns such as checkers, stripes, and any loud designs.

VISUAL SCHEDULE ACTIVITY

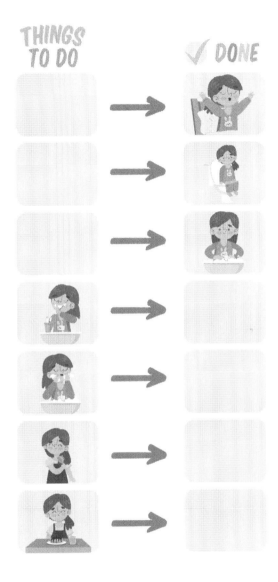

Select one of the suggested visual scheduling apps. Start with Choiceworks, which covers four main categories: Schedule, Waiting, Feelings, and Feelings Scale. One of the best things about using it to make a visual schedule is that it pairs scheduled activities with an "All Done" column, so you can check off every completed task. It also has timers that you can add to chosen tasks, as well as fully customizable schedules.

D: DEVELOPING A POSITIVE MINDSET

THE KEY TO BOOSTING YOUR CHILD'S SELF-ESTEEM

> *"Autism isn't something a person has, or a 'shell' that a person is trapped inside. There's no normal child hidden behind the autism. Autism is a way of being. It is pervasive; it colors every experience, every sensation, perception, thought, emotion, and encounter—every aspect of existence... Autism is not something that can be separated out from the person."*
>
> — JIM SINCLAIR (2012)

Studies have shown that Autistic kids who proudly accept their disorder are happier. Therefore, it is logical that this last component of the G.I.R.L.S. U.N.I.T.E.D. framework should focus on how to develop a positive mindset that will benefit your child and your family. It is logical to be taken aback when your child first receives their diagnosis and doctors start using words like "developmental delay" or mention possible conditions like "epilepsy." It can, indeed, be challenging to come to terms with a new reality that may differ from your original visions of parenthood.

In an emotive blog post, mom Mia Francis-Poulin (2019) recalls feeling overwhelmed when her son, who also had a host of other diagnoses (including oral dysphagia and bronchopulmonary dysplasia) was diagnosed with Autism. Many thoughts went through her mind; she wondered about a myriad of factors like whether her son would be able to live independently or speak, and whether he would ever be able to say "I love you." It wasn't long, however, before she decided that "Autism wasn't the end of the world, but an expansion of the world as we know it with its social rules and covenants." She knew that celebrating her son's Autism was the celebration of "a life won... a life that has meaning and purpose."

Loving your daughter unconditionally through the ups and downs that parenthood brings gives her the strongest tool she has for growing up confidently, with the knowledge that her life has meaning and that there are so many things she can achieve. Talking about Autism openly and sharing information that can help your child at school and in their social life is no different from talking about the sports they like or their interests. Autism is not something to hide but, rather, just another part of them.

HOW STIGMA CAN HARM AN AUTISTIC GIRL

The word "stigma" can be traced back to ancient Greece, where slaves, traitors, or criminals were literally branded to mark them permanently. Stigmatization is a deeply discrediting feature that makes people who experience it feel discounted and devalued.

In the case of Autism, stigmatization has a unique nature. This is because Autistic people look and behave like everyone else and we may communicate the way neurotypical people do. This can make it harder for others to realize that we are on the spectrum.

For many families, it can be particularly hard when a child who looks just like everyone else has a meltdown, because of how quick others are to judge. An Autistic child might ignore social rules, engage in echolalia, or invade someone else's space and the reaction can be swift and detrimental (Sarris 2022). One large-scale study (known as the SSC study) showed that around 75 percent of Autistic kids are left out of activities by other children often. Around 37 percent are teased for at least some of the time (Kinnear et al. 2015). Stigmatizing experiences include having difficulties making friends, being labeled by others as "weird," and being teased or insulted.

Sometimes, kids are teased because of their special interests. At other times, bullies can focus on a child's lack of focus or hyperfocus, or their non-social behavior. Parents report that stigmatization has negative effects on the whole family. Some state that the stress of bullying can reflect itself in similar behaviors from their Autistic child toward younger siblings.

The SSC study showed that these specific symptoms and behaviors often determine the frequency with which a child is rejected by others (from highest to lowest frequency):

- difficulties making eye contact
- getting upset when scheduling or routine changes occur
- stimming behaviors like hand flapping
- meltdowns
- getting aggressive toward others or threatening them
- having problems related to the bladder or bowel
- head-banging

The larger the number of these behaviors and the more frequent they are, the greater the chance of the child and their family being excluded or rejected by others. People who lack an awareness of Autism can mistake a child's behavior for poor parenting, mental illness, intellectual disability, or an explosive lack of control (Kennedy Krieger 2016).

Stigmatization reduces well-being in Autistic kids and increases masking behaviors (Turnock et al. 2022). One study (Botha et al. 2020) revealed that Autistic people consider their Autism to be "value-neutral." That means they consider their disorder to be just another feature they have, like their eye or hair color. However, in the study, participants considered that society sees their Autism as a negative trait to have. Their struggle is rooted in the difference between how they see themselves vs. how they feel society views them. Many are caught between telling others they are Autistic and hiding it, but they feel they are treated negatively anyway.

Media representations don't help, as they tend to present negative stereotypes of Autistic people as being withdrawn, awkward, or difficult. Studies have shown that 67 percent of media representations of Autism have stigmatizing cues. In some media, Autistic people are represented as unstable or unloved. These representations can make them feel like they have to mask so they are not judged. There are some positive representations, but they are fewer and further between. Of the ten stereotypes held about Autistic people, only two are positive: "high intelligence" and "special abilities" (think Sheldon Cooper and Rain Man). Stigma can lead many Autistic people to keep ASD a secret. In doing so, the stigma remains unchallenged and is propagated.

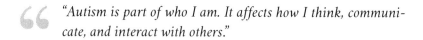

"Autism is part of who I am. It affects how I think, communicate, and interact with others."

— GINA, 19

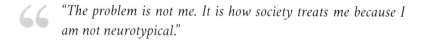

"The problem is not me. It is how society treats me because I am not neurotypical."

— PIPER, 29

> *"My brain is just wired differently. Being Autistic for me is like being good at art, being tall or short, being able to dance or not. Autism is not wrong or worse."*
>
> — SURI, 21

> *"I've met people who think everyone is on the spectrum to some extent, but I totally disagree. There are clear differences between Autistic and neurotypical people."*
>
> — EMMA, 37

> *"I always felt out of place and weird. My interest in nature is something that my classmates used to find strange or boring. Being diagnosed was a big relief because it gave me a new identity and I see it as a positive one."*
>
> — JULIA, 51

> *"I'm pretty good at masking so on the odd occasion that I have told people I'm Autistic, they sometimes don't believe it or tell me I can't really be Autistic. That is so annoying."*
>
> — ALEXIA, 23

> *"I do not use person-first language. I say 'I am Autistic' not 'I have Autism.' Autism is not a disease."*
>
> — PAM, 33

THE IMPORTANCE OF HOW A CHILD PERCEIVES HER AUTISM

When a child proudly owns their Autism, it impacts their lives profoundly, as found in numerous recent studies. One 2023 study on

Autistic teens aged fifteen to twenty-two (Cooper et al. 2023) showed that those who had a positive sense of their Autism identity and who felt solidarity with other Autistic people enjoyed better psychological well-being.

Even though the study participants were older than your child, right now, the findings highlight the importance of helping a child feel good about who they are and of encouraging them to form part of the Autism community. Developing a sense of pride about Autism gives those kids a vital mental health buffer that stands them in good stead when others tease or judge them. It is important to promote a balanced sense of Autism identity; one that includes its positive elements and its challenges. Kids can also benefit from post-diagnostic support, which helps them make sense of their diagnosis and tap into their strengths. As they grow into their teens, this can come in the form of social-identity-building programs, online settings where young Autistic people can come together, and stigma-reduction programs for non-Autistic youths. The stronger a child's sense of solidarity with the Autism community, the better their psychological well-being is likely to be. Advocacy is also key, since greater public awareness of the neurodiversity movement and making more connections with Autistic people is likely to reduce stigma.

Another study (Cooper et al. 2020) found that Autistic people who feel a strong sense of affiliation with other Autistic people, and who identify strongly as part of the community have higher self-esteem and psychological well-being. They also have lower depression and anxiety scores).

REFRAMING STEREOTYPES ABOUT AUTISTIC GIRLS

To reduce the impact that stigma can have on your child, start by reframing Autism. If your child knows that Autism means they are wired differently but that this does not make them any less valuable, interesting, smart, funny, or wonderful, their self-esteem can rise exponentially. If you can, try reframing Autism for others, too. There are many ways to be an advocate for Autism and to eliminate harmful myths and stereotypes. Advocating for your child at school can also make a big difference. By getting staff on your team and sharing important information with them, you can motivate them to be more active and embrace initiatives such as giving a talk to your daughter's class to explain what Autism is and what it feels like. More mature kids with Autism may wish to talk about what Autism is and explain the challenges and good things it brings.

There are many community groups, online forums, and apps you can use to connect with others and ensure you stay up to date with pertinent information, new resources, new initiatives, and similar. One good place to start is Arc—the nation's largest community-based organization advocating for people with intellectual and developmental disabilities. Arc has hundreds of state and local chapters across the country, each of which provides numerous services, support, and advocacy. Their website is www.arc.org.

Friend in Me is another fun social group that connects kids with disabilities and neurotypical kids through free online games and conversations via Zoom on a one-on-one basis every week. The buddies talk and play games for around forty-five minutes. This resource is for kids aged eight to eighteen. www.friendin megroup.com.

The Autism Project (TAP) offers social skills groups headed by speech-language pathologists, mental health practitioners, occupational therapists, and more, from ages five to young adulthood. www. theautismproject.org.

These are just a few of so many support groups that are free to join. Speak to other parents, conduct online searches, and meet up with people in your area. The amount of information you will receive is astounding, and you can do your share to pay it forward to the community, too.

EMBRACING A GROWTH MINDSET

A growth mindset differs from a fixed mindset in that it espouses that we are not born with a fixed set of skills and abilities. Instead, we can learn most skills we set our mind on, and utilize mistakes and "failures" as opportunities for growth. When you adopt a growth mindset, you celebrate others' wins, even when you "lose," because your failures do not define you. They simply allow you to refine your processes and hone your technique. Sometimes, they serve simply to show you that you aren't that keen on something and that you can pursue something else that fulfills you more.

Much research has been carried out on the growth mindset, an idea that was first coined by Stanford professor and psychologist Dr. Carol Dweck. As a teacher, Dweck noticed that some students bounced back fairly quickly from disappointments, while others seemed to be totally destroyed by even the smallest of setbacks. She also noticed that some students wanted at all costs to look "smart." They shied away from challenges because they believed that having to work hard at something meant they didn't have an innate ability. What's more, challenges involve a risk of failure... and failure could threaten their reputation as a "smart person" and, therefore, their identity. Those with a growth mindset, on the other hand, believed in the power of effort. They did not worry so much about "winning" and did not compare themselves to others, because they believed that everyone could pick up skills any time they set their mind to it.

The great thing about a growth mindset is that it can be developed by embracing five key characteristics: embracing learning, working hard, taking feedback constructively, welcoming challenges and opportunities to level up your skills, and using what you learn to improve your next attempt. The benefits of doing so are far-reaching. A growth mindset will help you throughout your parenting journey as it will boost your resilience, enhance your ability to adapt, motivate you, reduce stress, and open your mind to new information that may contradict preconceived ideas. Your daughter can also benefit greatly from seeing life as a series of adventures, some of which are enjoyed more than others. Some of these adventures can fascinate them forever; others may be left along the way in pursuit of new challenges (Diff not Less 2023). To encourage your daughter to embrace a growth mindset, you can:

- Create a supportive environment. Encourage your child to try the things and activities they are interested in, celebrating their efforts and achievements. Help them set realistic expectations and teach them how to break their goals into smaller steps. This way, you can have many mini-celebrations instead of just one.
- Embrace the word "yet." Using this word for things your child has not mastered helps them remain motivated and inspires them to be persistent.
- Feed your mind with affirming thoughts by focusing less on your shortcomings and more on your strengths and achievements, and encourage them to do the same. Take a leaf from the book of cognitive behavioral therapy. Encourage your kids to identify their negative thoughts and to think of past examples and experiences that can nip negative self-belief in the bud.
- Avoid comparisons.
- Give your child opportunities to belong to groups that enjoy the same interests and experiences they do.
- Encourage your child to identify the things they learn when they make mistakes. Sometimes, it may take days, weeks, or months to do so, so it can pay for them to write down their mistakes in a journal and revisit their entry later down the line. Doing so will make it easier to see how this mistake changed them for the better, refined their process, or taught them a new technique that has come in handy.
- Encourage your child to try new things and take healthy, reasoned risks. Trying new things allows you to make mistakes, discover new strengths, and focus on the journey

instead of the destination. Be the model of someone who embraces a "yes" mentality. Point out the many good things that happen when you say yes to an invitation or a new activity.

- Encourage positive behaviors such as active listening and turn-taking in your home. Active listening involves listening to understand, not just going through the motions to get your own point of view across. It can help to teach a child phrases like, "Oh, I see…" or "I can imagine how you feel," when someone is talking to them. Active listening is something that all of us hone as we mature, but it can help teach kids how to show someone you are interested in what they say by modeling this behavior with them and other family members.

- Share effective problem-solving skills. Show your child the four steps involved in effective problem-solving. These are:

    1. Identifying the problem. For instance: "Lisa did not invite me to her party."
    2. Brainstorming a few solutions together or with others. For instance: "I could call someone else to hang out with, spend time with my sibling on my special interest, have a family picnic," and more.
    3. Choosing one solution. "I think I will choose the last option, having a family picnic."
    4. Reflecting on the effectiveness of the solution. "We had fun, but next time I might call Jenny instead. She said she wanted to play with me, and I think she might be a nice new friend to have."

- As your child grows older, show them concrete examples of a growth vs. a fixed mindset. A few examples are provided in the table below:

Fixed Mindset	Growth Mindset
I'm just no good at this.	If I keep practicing this, I can get better at it.
When people tell me I've done something wrong or give me negative opinions about something I've done, I get angry.	I think about what people have told me to see if it can help me improve.
Popular people are lucky.	Popular people have good communication skills. I can learn those!
I wish I was as good at drawing as Marina.	I might ask Marina for a few drawing tips.
I feel embarrassed when I make mistakes.	That mistake was funny! But hey, now I know that I can do it better this way...
If I don't try hard things, I'll never fail.	Challenges help me grow and enjoy new activities and experiences.
When I fail, I give up.	When I fail, I try something else.
I can't do that.	I can't do that yet.

- Have a plan for dealing with setbacks. Have a few suggested activities for when your daughter feels sad or disappointed. You can try deep breathing, calming activities, and turning to the problem-solving method. You can also offer them support and validation, letting them know that they can find something positive even from a tough experience, even though what this is may not be visible yet.
- Talk to your child about positive role models like Temple Grandin. She has done so much to create inclusivity and to emphasize the many strengths that Autistic children and adults have.

REFRAMING THOUGHTS, EMOTIONS, AND BEHAVIORS

This cognitive behavioral therapy (CBT) exercise can help your child know themselves better, and know that they have many options when life throws curveballs their way. Use a journal to help your child reframe the way they see Autism (Autism Teaching Strategies n.d.).

1. Identify the emotion and draw how you felt.

> Example: *I felt upset when we didn't have playtime at school on Monday.* (Ask your child to draw how they felt. You can also show a picture of a body and ask your child to identify where they felt pain, tension, or discomfort. This will help your child identify when they are experiencing negative emotions earlier, so they can take action).

2. What thoughts did you have when you felt that way?

> Example: *I'm so tired of sitting here. I can't handle these changes. I'll be so exhausted I won't be able to finish my short story by tomorrow. I think the teacher changed the schedule just to upset me.*

3. What did you do when you felt that way?

> Example: *I started to cry.*

4. What did you say?

> Example: *I screamed that this was too much, and I wanted to play.*

5. To deal with upsetting thoughts, I could have tried these thoughts instead:

> Example: *I will make one last effort today. I understand the playground is being changed today so we cannot play outside.*

6. When I felt upset, I could have let someone know how I felt.

Example: *I could have told the teacher that changes are very hard for me and asked if I could have a short break.*

7. When I felt upset I could have done something differently.

Example: *I could have done a few breathing exercises or used my fidget toy.*

8. When I felt upset I could have calmed down my body by…

Example: *Washing my face with cool water, breathing, visualizing a peaceful place.*

Throughout this book, I have focused on the many things you can do to help your child embrace their Autism, go after their goals, and overcome challenges. In the last chapter, I will briefly touch on a few therapies and professionals that may make your journey easier.

THERAPIES AND PROFESSIONALS THAT CAN HELP YOU ALONG THE WAY

"*It takes a village to raise a child. It takes a child with autism to raise the consciousness of the village.*"

— ELAINE HALL (CIRCLE CARE SERVICES, N.D.)

I hope you can assemble a vibrant, helpful team that will enlighten you on useful strategies and empower your child. Let's start by taking a look at a few useful therapies that are currently in use. It is important to note that not all of these are scientifically proven to be successful, so talking to your child's team to formulate a plan that works for your child is key (Raising Children n.d.).

CURRENT THERAPIES

Sensory Integration Therapy

Sensory Integration Therapy was developed in the 1970s, to help children use all their senses (such as sight, sound, touch, smell, and taste) together. This therapy aims at tackling challenging behaviors that can be related to difficulties with processing sensory information.

This therapy begins with an assessment of the child by an occupational therapist. Next, the therapist creates a program that includes activities to bring about sensory responses, in particular, responses related to physical movement and balance. It might include bouncing, climbing, and swinging.

Sensory integration is not necessarily for everyone, as, to date, it has not been scientifically proven to be compatible with Autism. Some parents report positive results, while others find that it can increase their child's discomfort.

Applied Behavioral Analysis (ABA)

ABA, developed in the 1960s, relies on positive reinforcement and ABC (Antecedent, Behavior, Consequence) techniques. It aims to help Autistic children develop skills they are not acquiring on their own, and reduce harmful behaviors such as self-injury. ABA has received criticism from parents and Autism advocates. Its earliest form also included punishment and other aversive reinforcement methods, which are unacceptable, though current ABA does not use punishment. One of the most prevalent criticisms of modern ABA is that it is too hard on kids. Some parents feel that it involves considerable repetition, and the skills their kids learn don't necessarily transfer to other situations. Those who back this therapy, meanwhile, point out that it is often play-based and entertaining for kids.

Another major issue many parents and Autism advocates have with this therapy is its emphasis on getting kids to maintain eye contact or avoid stimming. For many, it essentially encourages masking behavior and gives kids the message that the way they naturally act and move must be changed (Lord 2023). Proponents of the therapy, meanwhile, argue that it does not aim to erase who a child is, but rather, to help them become more independent.

Relationship Development Intervention (RDI)

A family-based behavioral treatment that focuses on helping kids build social and emotional skills. Parents are trained to become their child's main therapist. RDI is based on the idea of "dynamic intelligence," or the ability to think flexibly and understand different perspectives, deal with change, and integrate multisensory information. Developed by clinical psychologists in the 1980s, it rests on honing a child's social skills so their quality of life improves.

Specific goals of RDI include sharing feelings and ideas, promoting sharing, solving problems creatively, reflecting on past experiences and talking about the future, and coping with uncertainty and obstacles (Raising Children n.d.). In RDI, a trained consultant develops an individualized program for kids, which parents use daily. Some research has shown that this treatment has positive results, but higher-quality studies are required.

Treatment and Education of Autistic and Related Communications Handicapped Children (TEACCH)

TEACCH is a therapy with a strong emphasis on physical structure, consistent schedules, establishing expectations, sticking to routines, and relying on visual-based cues. Developed in the 1960s, it is usually applied in a classroom-type setting, though parents can continue to use its techniques at home. Children have individualized visual schedules that they follow and as they become more skilled, the class becomes less structured, and they grow in independence. TEACCH is usually carried out by professionals such as speech therapists, special education teachers, or psychologists. Some research has shown positive effects from this therapy, but again, more high-quality studies would be useful.

Developmental, Individual Differences, Relationship-Based Approach (DIR)

This approach, commonly called "floor time," was developed in the 1980s. It promotes sensory development, motor skills, communication, and emotional and cognitive development, aiming to help kids reach specific milestones. It involves two to five hours of playtime between an adult and child and includes floor-time play, problem-solving interactions, and specialized activities. It starts with an assessment and includes school interactions, playdates, and therapies like speech and/or occupational therapy. Some studies have shown that DIR can improve kids' social and emotional development and hone the child-parent bond. More evidence is required on its effects on kids' communication and adaptive skills.

The Picture Exchange Communication System (PECS)

Earlier in the book, I briefly mentioned PECS. This is a visual-based approach that uses symbols instead of picture cards. Children learn to ask questions and communicate by using symbols instead of pictures. The therapy begins with the PECS trainer (which can be a parent or teacher) focusing on a child's favorite toys, foods, and similar. The child learns to swap these cards for the actual items they want. As they advance, kids can use the cards to ask for what they want, ask and answer questions, comment, and more. As they progress, they go from exchanging one card to building sentences using several cards at once. Research has shown that PECS can have positive effects on kids, particularly in terms of asking for things. More research is needed to see which kids respond best to PECS and to understand its effects on more complex communication.

Play Therapy

Play therapy involves getting down on the floor with an Autistic child to engage them through different types of play. Play therapists use toys to encourage children to communicate and build useful skills like turn-taking, using the imagination, and abstract thinking skills. As children make strides in the way they relate to others, the therapist might add more children into the session, to help develop more complex skills. If you are interested in play therapy, contact the Association for Play Therapy (APT), a national professional society comprising licensed mental health professionals. Play therapy is sometimes incorporated into specialized preschool programs or offered for free at local early intervention programs (Rudy 2023).

Music Therapy

Music therapy is used to help kids with verbal communication, initiating behavior, social interaction, sensory issues, cognition, motor skills, self-reliance, and anxiety reduction. Meta-studies have shown that the benefits of this type of therapy include increased social behavior, attention to tasks, vocabulary comprehension, verbalization, vocalization, communication, gesture, vocabulary, body awareness, coordination, and self-care skills. Music therapy can also help quell anxiety, while family-centered music therapy can help cement child-parent bonds. To find a music therapist for your child, look for someone with a Music Therapist-Board Certified (MT-BC) credential (Rudy 2023).

Animal-Assisted Therapy

Animals can have a calming effect on people with Autism, helping them deal with stress and avoid meltdowns. There are different types of animal therapy to opt for, including service dogs (which are professionally trained and certified to meet their person's needs), therapy animals (used during therapy sessions to facilitate openness and communication), family pets (who provide a source of unconditional love and support for kids at home), Autism emotional support animals (certified by a health professional as an emotional support animal), and equestrian therapy (involving riding and caring for horses). (Adult Ability Center n.d.).

Psychotherapeutic Options Involving Parents

Cognitive behavioral therapy (CBT) is considered to be an effective treatment for Autistic children experiencing mental health issues. Psychotherapists address the needs of Autistic kids and youth through methods such as using visual and concrete strategies, focusing on kids' special interests, tailoring treatment to the child's needs, and asking parents to participate. Parents can help with tasks such as helping kids complete their homework, modeling courageous behaviors, coaching their child to use coping strategies in their daily lives, and teaching kids through role-play. Parents can learn important strategies to motivate their kids to complete key tasks and provide emotional support to turn tasks into positive experiences for their child (Chan et al. 2023).

Medication

Sometimes, a child's team may recommend medications for symptoms like depression, insomnia, and difficulties with focusing. If kids have epilepsy (autistic people are more likely to develop epilepsy than those who are neurotypical), seizure medications may be recommended (Tuchman and Barker 2017).

Floor-Based Play Activity

The first step toward engaging in floor-based play is parallel play. To initiate it, enter your daughter's room or play area while she is playing with her toys. If she is playing with Lego, for instance, take a piece of Lego and do what she is with her pieces. At this stage, don't initiate conversation or interact with your child's toys. Just mimic what she is doing for around five minutes. Repeat this various times. At some point, when you leave, your child may follow you in an attempt to make you come back. This is a great sign that she is ready to open her play circle! Go back and play a bit more but continue copying what she is doing. After around four or five play sessions, your child may initiate play—for instance, by taking your Lego creation and adding a piece. Do what she suggests. Make an effort to avoid making any suggestions yourself. Keep playing this way until she asks you for an opinion. Don't be offended if she doesn't like what you propose. Remember that for this activity, she's the boss! (Ash n.d.).

BEFORE YOU GO

This book serves as the guide you turn to many times over as your child achieves her goals, meets new challenges, and knows the joy of self-confidence and self-love.

As you close its final pages, I imagine you getting ready to complete the activities at the end of every chapter and planning a host of play-dates and meetings. I hope you can take just a minute to share your thoughts on this book with other parents of Autistic girls who are seeking guidance on how to help their child achieve their personal, social, and academic goals.

Scan the QR code to leave your review.

Thanks for your help. May you have many moments of discovery, laughter, and love with your daughter.

Taylor Eberstadt

CONCLUSION

Congratulations on completing the G.I.R.L.S. U.N.I.T.E.D. journey; I hope you're already putting this multifaceted framework into motion and celebrating small and large achievements. At the start of this book, we looked at exactly what Autism is and what it isn't, focusing on how being on the spectrum affects different areas of your child's development—including skills like communication, language, and learning. We have also seen how Autism manifests itself very differently in girls than in boys, thus often leading to misdiagnosis or late diagnosis.

We have discovered how wide the Autism spectrum is: how it impacts kids and families very differently, and benefits from having an open mind and a willingness to understand and adapt to a child's needs. The impact of Autism also varies depending on which concurrent conditions a child may have, some of the most common of which are ADHD, BPD, depression, and anxiety. We saw how mindfulness can help tackle the symptoms of anxiety and depression, boosting children's resilience to the stressors of everyday life at school, at home, and with friends.

We looked into the pros and cons of receiving an early diagnosis. Some parents fear that their children will be stigmatized and labeled if they are diagnosed. Many others espouse the numerous benefits of an early diagnosis, including being able to find help immediately from occupational, speech, and other therapists. Many parents breathe a sigh of relief when they finally confirm their intuition that their child is Autistic. A diagnosis means they no longer need to feel like their child's behavior is the result of something they are "doing wrong." It can be so tough when others judge a meltdown or other behaviors as resulting from "bad parenting." That couldn't be further from the truth.

We delved deep into kids' sensory challenges, explaining why stopping a child from stimming can be detrimental to their well-being. We also offered solutions to help kids deal with sensory overload, such as making adaptations to the family home and ensuring kids have a quiet space to call their own.

I explained how sensory and learning issues often overlap. Kids who are struggling to deal with so many sights, sounds, and changes to their routine can find it incredibly difficult to focus, remember sequences, and communicate what they know. Special interests take on special importance in this realm, since they enable kids to shine and become veritable experts in their chosen areas—and this provides a vital boost for their self-esteem. I also mentioned many tools that can keep kids on track, including visuals, task sheets, and apps.

For much of this book, I stressed the importance of meeting kids where they are—letting them take the lead, so to speak. In Chapter Six, which was centered on communication, we saw that instead of aiming for perfection, it helps to aim for understanding. We encountered fascinating stories of kids who created entirely new means of communication that their loving families discovered, learned, and utilized with their children, with wonderful results.

Understanding Autism empowers you to see beyond behaviors that can, indeed, be very challenging at times—especially when you're tired. Factors such as alexithymia and sensory difficulties can make it so tough for kids to regulate their emotions. When they have a meltdown or simply do not hear or process what you have asked them to do, it's not that they don't want to be helpful; often, they simply can't.

Making friends is one of the biggest hurdles for Autistic kids, which is why providing them with as many opportunities as possible to make and sustain friendships is a great investment of time. Kids are more likely to connect with those with shared interests. Many studies have shown that they find connecting with other Autistic kids particularly fulfilling. We also discussed the importance of forming part of a community and advocating for Autism. People who feel a strong sense of affiliation with other Autistic people, and who have positive views about the Autistic community enjoy better psychological well-being.

We ended with the growth mindset and its many benefits for your child and yourself. You don't always have to get things right from the start and, in fact, you may start and stop many approaches, deciding they are not for you. That is perfectly okay. There is so much to be gained from our mistakes, and many would say they are our greatest teachers. The final chapter of this book lists popular therapies and professionals. Speech therapists, occupational therapists, and psychotherapists are three vital professionals, many of whom put heart and soul into knowing your child's needs and helping them thrive in so many ways.

All that is left, then, is my best wishes for you, the parent of a marvelous girl: her best friend and strongest advocate. Thank you for reading my stories and experiences and the results of my research. Autism is my special interest and if my Autistic students and friends have taught me one thing, it is how resilient and creative we are. We grow stronger when our friends and loved ones believe in us and allow us to be who we are, without making us feel like we have to mask to be valuable.

I wish you many hours watching your child delve deeply into interests, some of which may last for days, while others are their lifelong companions. I wish you the joy and laughter that arises when your child says or does something unexpected—those bolt-in-the-blue moments of magic. And I hope that amid so much learning, growth, and advocacy, you find time for yourself. You are doing a magnificent job; the level of your commitment to your child is something few people may understand completely. But there is someone who feels your love, dedication, and devotion deeply: your daughter. Cherish her and surround her with people who love her just as she is.

REFERENCES

Adult Ability Center. "Animal-Assisted Autism Therapy: The Social, Emotional, and Physical Benefits." Accessed May 5, 2024. https://adultautismcenter.org/blog/animal-therapy-for-autism/.

Aherne, Anita. 2023. "Why Girls with Autism Face Unique Anxiety Challenges—Living on the Spectrum." Living on the Spectrum. May 21, 2023. https://www.livingonthespectrum.com/health-and-wellbeing/why-girls-with-autism-face-unique-anxiety-challenges/.

Arizona Autism United. "Benefits of Speech Therapy for Children with Autism." August 2021. https://azaunited.org/blog/benefits-of-speech-therapy-for-children-with-autism.

Aruma. "Quotes about Autism." Accessed May 13, 2024. https://www.aruma.com.au/about-us/blog/quotes-about-autism/

Ash. "Activities for Autistic Children." Autism 360. Accessed May 5, 2024. https://www.autism360.com/activities-for-autistic-children.

Attwood, Tony. *The Complete Guide to Asperger's Syndrome*. London and Philadelphia: Jessica Kingsley Publishers, 2007.

Autism Awareness Australia. "Women and Girls." Accessed May 1, 2024. https://www.autismawareness.com.au/understanding-autism/women-girls.

Autism Learning Partners. "Understanding the Diagnostic Evaluation Process for Autism Spectrum Disorder." Autism Learning Partners. Accessed April 10, 2024. https://www.autismlearningpartners.com/understanding-the-diagnostic-evaluation-process-for-autism-spectrum-disorder.

Autism Speaks. "How General Education Teachers Can Support Students with ASD." Accessed April 2, 2024. https://www.autismspeaks.org/blog/how-general-education-teachers-can-support-students-asd.

Autism Teaching Strategies. "Simple CBT Worksheets." Accessed May 3, 2024. https://autismteachingstrategies.com/wp-content/uploads/2013/05/CBT-Worksheets-Sets.pdf.

Autism Together. "Sight." Accessed April 2, 2024. https://www.autismtogether.co.uk/autism-and-the-seven-senses-sight/.

Bargiela, Sarah, Robyn Steward, and William Mandy. "The Experiences of Late-diagnosed Women with Autism Spectrum Conditions: An Investigation of the Female Autism Phenotype." *Journal of Autism and Developmental Disorders* 46, no. 10 (July 2016): 3281–94. https://doi.org/10.1007/s10803-016-2872-8.

Bernard, Sallie. "8 Critical Measures to Counter Suicide." Autism Speaks. April, 2013. https://www.autismspeaks.org/blog/8-critical-measures-counter-suicide.

Botha, Monique, Bridget Dibb, and David M. Frost. "'Autism Is Me': An Investigation of

How Autistic Individuals Make Sense of Autism and Stigma." *Disability & Society* 37, no. 3 (October 2020): 427–53. https://doi.org/10.1080/09687599.2020.1822782.

Carmassi, Claudia, Laura Palagini, Danila Caruso, Isabella Masci, Lino Nobili, Antonio Vita, and Liliana Dell'Osso. "Systematic Review of Sleep Disturbances and Circadian Sleep Desynchronization in Autism Spectrum Disorder: Toward an Integrative Model of a Self-Reinforcing Loop." *Frontiers in Psychiatry* 10 (June 2019). https://doi.org/10.3389/fpsyt.2019.00366.

Cazalis, Fabienne, Elisabeth Reyes, Séverine Leduc, and David Gourion. "Evidence That Nine Autistic Women Out of Ten Have Been Victims of Sexual Violence." *Frontiers in Behavioral Neuroscience* 16 (April 2022). https://doi.org/10.3389/fnbeh.2022.852203.

CHADD. "ADHD and Autism Spectrum Disorder." Accessed May 1, 2024. https://chadd.org/about-adhd/adhd-and-autism-spectrum-disorder.

Chan, Victoria, Carly Albaum, Nazilla Khanlou, Henny A. Westra, and Jonathan A. Weiss. "Parent Involvement in Mental Health Treatment for Autistic Children: A Grounded Theory-Informed Qualitative Analysis." *Child Psychiatry and Human Development* (October 2023). https://doi.org/10.1007/s10578-023-01621-x.

Cherry, Kendra. "What Is Attachment Theory?." Verywell Mind. February 22, 2023. https://www.verywellmind.com/what-is-attachment-theory-2795337.

Cincinnati Children's. "Pragmatic Language." Accessed April 2, 2024. https://www.cincinnatichildrens.org/-/media/Cincinnati-Childrens/Home/service/s/speech/hcp/doctor-info/information-language-PDF-pragmatic-lan-6.pdf.

Circle Care Services. "20 Inspiring Quotes about Autism Every Parent Must Read Today." Accessed May 4, 2024. https://circlecareservices.com/20-quotes-about-autism-and-parenting/.

Conner, Caitlin M., Josh Golt, Rebecca C. Shaffer, Giulia Righi, Matthew Siegel, and Carla A. Mazefsky. "Emotion Dysregulation Is Substantially Elevated in Autism Compared to the General Population: Impact on Psychiatric Services." *Autism Research* 14, no. 1 (January 2021): 169–81. https://doi.org/10.1002/aur.2450.

Cook, Jennifer, Laura Hull, and William Mandy. "Improving Diagnostic Procedures in Autism for Girls and Women: A Narrative Review." *Neuropsychiatric Disease and Treatment* 20 (May 2023): 505–14. https://doi.org/10.2147/ndt.s372723.

Cooper, Kate, Ailsa Russell, Jiedi Lei, and Laura Smith. "The Impact of a Positive Autism Identity and Autistic Community Solidarity on Social Anxiety and Mental Health in Autistic Young People." *Autism* 27, no. 3 (April 2023): 848–57. https://doi.org/10.1177/13623613221118351.

Cooper, Rosalind, Kate Cooper, Ailsa J. Russell, and Laura G.E. Smith. "'I'm Proud to be a Little Bit Different': The Effects of Autistic Individuals' Perceptions of Autism and Autism Social Identity on Their Collective Self-esteem." *Journal of Autism and Developmental Disorders* 51 (June 2020): 704–704. https://doi.org/10.1007/s10803-020-04575-4.

Costello, Rachel. "Yoga Sensory Activities for Autism (Using the Three M's!)." Yo Re Mi Kids. October 1, 2019. https://www.yoremikids.com/news/yoga-sensory-activities-for-autism.

Counselling for Kids. "Anger Statistics." Accessed March 2, 2024. https://www.coun sellingforkids.co.uk/anger-statistics.

Crompton, Catherine J., Sonny Hallett, Danielle Ropar, Emma Flynn, and Sue Fletcher-Watson. "'I Never Realised Everybody Felt as Happy as I Do When I Am around Autistic People': A Thematic Analysis of Autistic Adults' Relationships with Autistic and Neurotypical Friends and Family." *Autism* 24, no. 6 (March 2020): 1438–48. https://doi.org/10.1177/1362361320908976.

Davis, Paige E., Jessica Slater, David C. Marshall, and Diana L. Robins. "Autistic Children Who Create Imaginary Companions: Evidence of Social Benefits." *Autism* 27, no. 1 (January 2023): 244–52. https://doi.org/10.1177/13623613221092195.

Delano, Claire. "Benefits of Sign Language for Autism." Autism Parenting. November 16, 2023. https://www.autismparentingmagazine.com/autistic-child-sign-language/.

Diff not Less. "Empower Your Child with Autism: Unlocking the Power of a Growth Mindset." June 10, 2023. https://diffnotless.com/blogs/blog/teach-child-autism-growth-mindset.

Digitale, Erin. "Hyperconnectivity Found in Brains of Children with Autism, Study Says." Stanford Medicine. June 26, 2013. https://med.stanford.edu/news/all-news/2013/06/hyperconnectivity-found-in-brains-of-children-with-autism-study-says.html.

DiMare, Deborah. "5 Interior Design Tips on Autism." Vegan Design. June 14, 2023. https://www.vegandesign.org/blog/interior-design-for-autism.

Dreison, Kimberly. "A Brief Overview of the ADOS-2: An Assessment for Autism Spectrum Disorder." Children's Resource Group. Accessed April 15, 2024. https://www.childrensresourcegroup.com/a-brief-overview-of-the-ados-2-an-assessment-for-autism-spectrum-disorder/.

Egber, Merrick. "30 Quotes from 30 People with Autism." Ernie Els. April 6, 2021. https://www.elsforautism.org/30-quotes-from-30-people-with-autism.

Emily. "Alexithymia and Autism." Autistic Girls Network. Accessed April 3, 2024. https://autisticgirlsnetwork.org/alexithymia-and-autism/.

Fox, Alex Ashley. "The Economic and Emotional Costs of Autistic Masking." January 20, 2023. The Century Foundation. https://tcf.org/content/commentary/the-economic-and-emotional-costs-of-autistic-masking/.

Francis-Poulin, Mia. "Why I Celebrate My Son's Autism." Collin County Moms. April 15, 2019. https://collincounty.momcollective.com/parenting/why-i-celebrate-my-sons-autism/.

Functional Medicine. "Food Allergies Connection with Autism/ADHD/ASD." May 26, 2022. https://www.functionalmedicineclinic.in/post/food-allergies-connection-with-autism-adhd-asd.

Furfaro, Hannah. 2018. "Autistic Children Prone to Food, Skin and Respiratory Allergies." The Transmitter. July 25, 2018. https://www.spectrumnews.org/news/autistic-children-prone-food-skin-respiratory-allergies/.

Garnett, Michelle, and Attwood, Tony. "How to Recognise Autism in Girls." Attwood and Garnett Events. Accessed May 6, 2024. https://attwoodandgarnettevents.com/how-to-recognise-autism-in-girls/.

Goddard, Helen, and Anna Cook. 2021. "'I Spent Most of Freshers in My Room'—A Qualitative Study of the Social Experiences of University Students on the Autistic Spectrum." *Journal of Autism and Developmental Disorders* 52, no. 6 (2022): 2701–16. https://doi.org/10.1007/s10803-021-05125-2.

Grandin, Temple. *Thinking in Pictures*. London: Bloomsbury, 2006.

Grogan, Alisha. "7 Yoga Poses to Calm Kids Down FAST!." Your Kids Table. November 7, 2023. https://yourkidstable.com/calming-yoga-for-kids/.

Guo, Xiaonan, Tiago Simas, Meng-Chuan Lai, Michael Lombardo, Bhismadev Chakrabarti, Amber Ruigrok, Edward T. Bullmore, Simon Baron-Cohen, Huafu Chen, and John Suckling. "Enhancement of Indirect Functional Connections with Shortest Path Length in the Adult Autistic Brain." *Human Brain Mapping* 40, number 18 (August 2019): 5354–69. https://doi.org/10.1002/hbm.24777.

Hands Center for Autism. "Why Change Is Hard for Children with Autism." January 25, 2024. https://www.handscenter.com/why-change-is-hard-for-children-with-autism.

Hartley, Sigan L., and Darryn M. Sikora. "Sex Differences in Autism Spectrum Disorder: An Examination of Developmental Functioning, Autistic Symptoms, and Coexisting Behavior Problems in Toddlers." *Journal of Autism and Developmental Disorders* 39, no. 12 (July 2009): 1715–22. https://doi.org/10.1007/s10803-009-0810-8.

Hellings, Jessica, and Andrea Witwer. "Autism and Bipolar Disorder." Autism Speaks. Accessed April 15, 2024. https://www.autismspeaks.org/expert-opinion/autism-bipolar.

Hendrickx, Sarah. *Women and Girls with Autism Spectrum Disorder: Understanding Life Experiences from Early Childhood to Old Age*. London and Philadelphia: Jessica Kingsley Publishers, 2015.

Hendrickx, Sarah. "Anxiety and Autism in the Classroom." June 19, 2018. https://www.autism.org.uk/advice-and-guidance/professional-practice/anxiety-classroom.

Kalyani, Bangalore G., Ganesan Venkatasubramanian, Rashmi Arasappa, Naren P. Rao, Sunil V. Kalmady, Rishikesh V. Behere, H.V. Rajanarsing Rao, M.K. Vasudev, and Bangalore N. Gangadhar. "Neurohemodynamic Correlates of 'OM' Chanting: A Pilot Functional Magnetic Resonance Imaging Study." *International Journal of Yoga/International Journal of Yoga* 4, number 1 (January 2011): 3. https://doi.org/10.4103/0973-6131.78171.

Kennedy Krieger Institute. "Families Face Autism Stigma, Isolation." February 4, 2016. https://www.kennedykrieger.org/stories/interactive-autism-network-ian/families-face-autism-stigma-isolation.

Kinnear, Sydney H., Bruce G. Link, Michelle Sondra Ballan, and Ruth L. Fischbach. "Understanding the Experience of Stigma for Parents of Children with Autism Spectrum Disorder and the Role Stigma Plays in Families' Lives." *Journal of Autism and Developmental Disorders* 46, no. 3 (December 2015): 942–53. https://doi.org/10.1007/s10803-015-2637-9.

Knickmeyer, Rebecca, Sally Wheelwright, and Simon Baron-Cohen. "Sex-Typical Play: Masculinization/Defeminization in Girls with an Autism Spectrum Condition." *Journal of Autism and Developmental Disorders* 38, no. 6 August 2008): 1028–35. https://doi.org/10.1007/s10803-007-0475-0.

Kuo, Melissa H, Gael I. Orsmond, Wendy J. Coster, and Ellen S. Cohn. "Media Use among Adolescents with Autism Spectrum Disorder." *Autism* 18, no. 8 (October 2013): 914–23. https://doi.org/10.1177/1362361313497832.

Laber-Warren, Emily. "The Benefits of Special Interests in Autism." The Transmitter. May 12, 2021. https://www.spectrumnews.org/features/deep-dive/the-benefits-of-special-interests-in-autism/.

Leclerc, Emily. "New Research First to Test 60-Year-Old Theory on Autism." Waisman Center. March 28, 2024. https://www.waisman.wisc.edu/2024/03/28/new-research-first-to-test-60-year-old-theory-on-autism/.

Lesley University. " The Psychology of Emotional and Cognitive Empathy." Accessed April 16, 2024. https://lesley.edu/article/the-psychology-of-emotional-and-cognitive-empathy.

Libster, Natalie, Azia Knox, Selin Engin, Daniel H. Geschwind, Julia Parish-Morris, and Connie Kasari. "Sex Differences in Friendships and Loneliness in Autistic and Non-Autistic Children across Development." *Molecular Autism* 14, no. 1 (February 2023). https://doi.org/10.1186/s13229-023-00542-9.

Little Puddins. "Autism APPs for Communication & Visual Schedules." Accessed May 1, 2024. https://littlepuddins.ie/communication-visual-schedule-apps.

Lord, Catherine. "The Controversy around ABA." Child Mind Institute. November 6, 2023. https://childmind.org/article/controversy-around-applied-behavior-analysis/.

Lovering, Cathy. "Autism in Kids: Why Is Early Diagnosis Important?" Psych Central. November 16, 2022. https://psychcentral.com/autism/early-diagnosis-of-autism.

Mann, Denise. "Among Kids with Autism, Girls Are More Prone to Anxiety Disorders than Boys." US News. May 3, 2023. https://www.usnews.com/news/health-news/articles/2023-05-03/among-kids-with-autism-girls-are-more-prone-to-anxiety-disorders-than-boys.

Marcus Autism Center. "Autism Habits—When to Worry." Accessed May 1, 2024. https://www.marcus.org/autism-resources/autism-tips-and-resources/eating-habits-when-to-worry.

Marschall, Amy. "AuDHD: When Autism and ADHD Co-Occur." VeryWell Mind. February 20, 2024. https://www.verywellmind.com/what-to-know-about-comorbid-autism-and-adhd-6944530.

McAllister, Nick. 2020. "Masking When You Have Autism Can Help You Blend in, but You Might Not Be Doing Yourself Any Favours." ABC News, December 19, 2020. https://www.abc.net.au/news/2020-12-20/masking-when-you-have-autism-is-more-common-than-you-think---an/12999102.

McDougle, Christopher. "Autism and Depression: What Is the Connection?" Autism Speaks. Accessed May 6, 2024. https://www.autismspeaks.org/expert-opinion/autism-depression.

Meyer, Sara. "Friendship May Look Different for Autistic People." Altogether Autism Takiwatanga. Accessed April 1, 2024. https://www.altogetherautism.org.nz/friend ship-may-look-different-for-autistic-people/.

Miller, Stuart. "It Took a Woman with Autism 25 Years to Find Her Voice. Now She's Telling Her Story." Washington Post. April 9, 2021. https://www.washingtonpost. com/entertainment/books/it-took-a-woman-with-autism-25-years-to-find-her-voice-now-shes-telling-her-story/2021/04/07/22b5e316-97a4-11eb-a6d0-13d207aadb78_story.html.

Moller, Ralph. "Benefits of Sign Language for Autism." Above & Beyond Therapy. January 23, 2024. https://www.abtaba.com/blog/sign-language-for-autism.

Mongina, Night. "Inspirational Autism Quotes for Strength and Understanding." Legit. March 9, 2024. https://www.legit.ng/ask-legit/quotes-messages/1581040-inspira tional-autism-quotes-strength-understanding/.

Moore, Marissa. "Are There Differences between Autistic Boys and Girls?" Psych Central. October 17, 2023. https://psychcentral.com/autism/comparison-of-boys-and-girls-living-with-autism-spectrum-disorder.

National Autistic Society. "Autism Seminar with Sarah Hendrickx." March 2, 2019. https://www.shantsnas.org.uk/seminar.

National Autistic Society, "Meltdowns." Accessed April 2, 2024. https://www.autism. org.uk/advice-and-guidance/topics/behaviour/meltdowns/all-audiences.

National Institute on Deafness and Other Communication Disorders. "Autism Spectrum Disorder: Communication Problems in Children." Accessed May 12, 2024. https://www.nidcd.nih.gov/health/autism-spectrum-disorder-communica tion-problems-children.

Neff, Megan Anna. "ASD And ADHD Nervous System." Insights of a Neurodivergent Clinician. September 13, 2023. https://neurodivergentinsights.com/blog/autistic-adhd-nervous-system.

Notbohm, Ellen. Ten Things Every Child with Autism Wishes You Knew: Revised and Updated. 2019.

Nowell, Kerri P., Courtney J. Bernardin, Cynthia E. Brown, and Stephen M. Kanne. "Characterization of Special Interests in Autism Spectrum Disorder: A Brief Review and Pilot Study Using the Special Interests Survey." Journal of Autism and Developmental Disorders 51, no. 8 (September 2020): 2711–24. https://doi.org/10. 1007/s10803-020-04743-6.

Okoye, Chiugo, Chidi M. Obialo-Ibeawuchi, Omobolanle A. Obajeun, Sarosh Sarwar, Christine Maher Fouad Tawfik, Madeeha Subhan Waleed, Asad Ullah Wasim, Iman Mohamoud, Adebola Yewande Afolayan, and Rheiner N. Mbaezue. "Early Diagnosis of Autism Spectrum Disorder: A Review and Analysis of the Risks and Benefits." Cureus (August 2023). https://doi.org/10.7759/cureus.43226.

Önal, Seda, Monika Sachadyn-Król, and Małgorzata Kostecka. "A Review of the Nutritional Approach and the Role of Dietary Components in Children with Autism Spectrum Disorders in Light of the Latest Scientific Research." Nutrients 15, number 23 (November 2023): 4852. https://doi.org/10.3390/nu15234852.

Parent Press. "Quotes About Autism: Spreading Awareness, Understanding, and

Acceptance Through Powerful Messages." April 30, 2024. https://getgoally.com/blog/20-quotes-about-autism-that-we-love/.

Parsons, Marissa A. "Autism Diagnosis in Females by Eating Disorder Professionals." *Journal of Eating Disorders* 11, no. 1 (May 2023). https://doi.org/10.1186/s40337-023-00785-0.

Pittsburgh Center for Autistic Advocacy. "FAQ." Accessed May 6, 2024. https://autisticpcgh.org/faq/.

Price, Devon. *Unmasking Autism: Discovering the New Faces of Neurodiversity*. Arlington: Future Horizons Inc., 2022.

Raising Children. "Autism Therapies Guide." Accessed May 4, 2024. https://raisingchildren.net.au/autism/therapies-guide/dir-floortime-model.

Raising Children. "Child Sexual Abuse: Keeping Autistic Children and Teenagers Safe." Accessed April 1, 2024. https://raisingchildren.net.au/autism/health-wellbeing/autism-child-sexual-abuse/child-sexual-abuse-keeping-autistic-children-teens-safe.

Raising Children. "Conditions That Can Occur with Autism." Accessed May 1, 2024. https://raisingchildren.net.au/autism/learning-about-autism/about-autism/conditions-that-occur-with-asd.

Raising Children. "Relationship Development Intervention (RDI)." Accessed May 4, 2024. https://raisingchildren.net.au/autism/therapies-guide/rdi-.

Raising Children. "Sleep Problems and Solutions: Autistic Children." Accessed May 4, 2024. https://raisingchildren.net.au/autism/health-wellbeing/sleep/sleep-problems-children-with-asd.

Raising Children. "Starting Primary School: Autistic Children." Accessed April 1, 2024. https://raisingchildren.net.au/autism/school-play-work/autism-spectrum-disorder-primary-school/starting-primary-school-asd.

Rivera-Bonet, Charlene N. "Sensory Responses in Autistic Children Are Linked to a Small Under-Explored Region Tucked Deep Down in the Brain Called the Brainstem." Waisman Center. April 5, 2023. https://www.waisman.wisc.edu/2023/04/05/sensory-responses-in-autistic-children.

Roberts, Andrea L., Karestan C. Koenen, Kristen Lyall, Elise B. Robinson, and Marc G. Weisskopf. "Association of Autistic Traits in Adulthood With Childhood Abuse, Interpersonal Victimization, and Posttraumatic Stress." Child Abuse & Neglect 45 (July 2015): 135–42. https://doi.org/10.1016/j.chiabu.2015.04.010.

Rosson, Haley, and Penny Pennington Weeks. "'I Am Different, Not Less': Temple Grandin and Strengths-Based Leadership Education." *Journal of Leadership Education* 17, no. 3 (2018): 231–40. https://doi.org/10.12806/v17/i3/a4.

Rudy, Lisa Jo. "Benefits of Play Therapy and Autism." VeryWell Health. July 28, 2023. https://www.verywellhealth.com/play-therapy-and-autism-the-basics-260059.

Rudy, Lisa Jo. "How Speech Therapy Benefits Autistic Children." VeryWell Health. March 21, 2024. https://www.verywellhealth.com/speech-therapy-for-autism-the-basics-260577.

Rudy, Lisa Jo. "Music Therapy for Autism." VeryWell Health. December 14, 2023. https://www.verywellhealth.com/music-therapy-for-autism-260057.

Rudy, Lisa Jo. "The Connection between Bipolar Disorder and Autism: What to Know."

VeryWell Health. May 2, 2024. https://www.verywellhealth.com/bipolar-disorder-and-autism-5204652.

Rudy, Lisa Jo. "The Link Between Autism and Sleep Issues." VeryWell Health. August 4, 2023 https://www.verywellhealth.com/autism-and-sleep-issues-41658.

Rudy, Lisa Jo. "Visual Thinking and Autism." VeryWell Health. October 25, 2023. https://www.verywellhealth.com/visual-thinking-and-autism-5119992.

Ruggieri, Victor. "Autism, Depression, and Risk of Suicide." *Medicina* 80, Suppl 2 (2020): 12–16. https://pubmed.ncbi.nlm.nih.gov/32150706/.

Sarris, Marina. "Autism, Meltdowns, and the Struggle to Manage Emotions." Spark. March 24, 2022. https://sparkforautism.org/discover_article/managing-emotions/.

Sarris, Marina. "The Stigma of Autism: When Everyone is Staring at You." April 5, 2022. https://sparkforautism.org/discover_article/stigma-autism/.

Schumer, Lizz. "14 Powerful Quotes about Autism." Good Housekeeping. February 21, 2024. https://www.goodhousekeeping.com/life/a43118585/quotes-about-autism/.

Schwartz, Sophie. "Auditory Processing Disorder." Autism Speaks. Accessed May 6, 2024. https://www.autismspeaks.org/expert-opinion/auditory-processing-disorder.

Shalev, Ido, Varun Warrier, David M. Greenberg, Paula Smith, Carrie Allison, Simon Baron-Cohen, Alal Eran, and Florina Uzefovsky. 2022. "Reexamining Empathy in Autism: Empathic Disequilibrium as a Novel Predictor of Autism Diagnosis and Autistic Traits." *Autism Research* 15, no. 10 (March 2022): 1917–28. https://doi.org/10.1002/aur.2794.

Sinclair, Jim. "Don't Mourn for Us." *Autonomy, the Critical Journal of Interdisciplinary Autism Studies* 1, no. 1 (October 3, 2012): 211–220. https://doi.org/10.1007/978-981-13-8437-0_15.

Skoog, Thérése, and Sevgi Bayram Özdemir. "Explaining Why Early-Maturing Girls Are More Exposed to Sexual Harassment in Early Adolescence." *Journal of Early Adolescence* 36, no. 4 (January 2015): 490–509. https://doi.org/10.1177/0272431614568198.

Smith, Adam. "The Empathy Imbalance Hypothesis of Autism: A Theoretical Approach to Cognitive and Emotional Empathy in Autistic Development." *The Psychological Record*, 59, no. 2 (June 2017), 273–294. https://doi.org/10.1007/BF03395663.

Stamurai. "15 Speech Therapy Exercises for Children with Autism." September 22, 2021. https://stamurai.com/blog/speech-therapy-exercises-for-children-with-autism/.

Stewart, Jan. "30 Quotes to Celebrate Autism Acceptance Month." April 1, 2024. Today's Parent. https://www.todaysparent.com/family/special-needs/quotes-to-celebrate-autism-acceptance-month.

Suskind, Ron. *Life, Animated : a Story of Sidekicks, Heroes, and Autism.* New York: Kingswell, 2014.

The Spectrum. "Diets for Autistic People." Accessed May 2, 2024. https://thespectrum.org.au/autism-support-services/professionals/dietitians/.

Tobik, Amy. "Quotes about Autism." August 5, 2021. Autism Parenting. https://www.autismparentingmagazine.com/quotes-about-autism/.

Tuchman, Roberto, and Angela Barker. "Epilepsy and Autism." National Autistic Society. July 27, 2017. https://www.autism.org.uk/advice-and-guidance/profes sional-practice/epilepsy-autism.

Turnock, Alice, Kate Langley, and Catherine R. G. Jones. "Understanding Stigma in Autism: A Narrative Review and Theoretical Model." *Autism in Adulthood* 4, no. 1 (March 2022): 76–91. https://doi.org/10.1089/aut.2021.0005.

UCLA Health. "Brain Changes in Autism Are Far More Sweeping than Previously Known, UCLA-Led Study Finds." November 2, 2022. https://www.uclahealth.org/ news/release/brain-changes-autism-are-far-more-sweeping-previously-known.

Understood. "The Difference Between IEPs and 504 Plans." Accessed March 18, 2024. https://www.understood.org/en/articles/the-difference-between-ieps-and-504-plans.

USDA My Plate. "Resources." Accessed May 22, 2024. https://www.myplate.gov/ resources.

Westwood, Heather, Jess Kerr-Gaffney, Daniel Ståhl, and Kate Tchanturia. "Alexithymia in Eating Disorders: Systematic Review and Meta-Analyses of Studies Using the Toronto Alexithymia Scale." *Journal of Psychosomatic Research* 99 (August 2017): 66–81. https://doi.org/10.1016/j.jpsychores.2017.06.007.

Westwood, Heather, William Mandy, and Kate Tchanturia. "Clinical Evaluation of Autistic Symptoms in Women with Anorexia Nervosa." *Molecular Autism* 8, no. 1 (March 2017). https://doi.org/10.1186/s13229-017-0128-x.

Wieckowski, Andrea Trubanova, Stephanie Luallin, Zhaoxing Pan, Giulia Righi, Robin L. Gabriels, and Carla A. Mazefsky. "Gender Differences in Emotion Dysregulation in an Autism Inpatient Psychiatric Sample." *Autism Research* 13, no. 8 (March 2020): 1343–48. https://doi.org/10.1002/aur.2295.

Williams, Kym. "Autism: Managing Over-Stimulation and Stress." Canopy Children's Solutions. April 30, 2020. https://mycanopy.org/2020/04/over-stimulation-stress/.

Williamson, Eric. "The Road to $532 Million: Why Are Boys Diagnosed with Autism More than Girls?" UVA Today. December 1, 2023. https://news.virginia.edu/ content/road-532-million-why-do-girls-avoid-autism-more-often-boys.

Winter-Messiers, Mary Ann. 2007. "From Tarantulas to Toilet Brushes." *Remedial and Special Education* 28, no. 3 (May 2007): 140–52. https://doi.org/10.1177/ 07419325070280030301.

Zauderer, Steven. "Autism Routines: Why Children with ASD Like Routines." Cross River Therapy. September 19, 2023. https://www.crossrivertherapy.com/autism/ routines.

Zauderer, Steven. "The Double Empathy Problem in Autism, Explained." Cross River Therapy. September 18, 2023. https://www.crossrivertherapy.com/autism/double-empathy-problem.

Made in United States
Troutdale, OR
11/07/2024

24553100R00123